L

JENNIFER TOO

FORTUNE & FENG SHUI

Tiger 2019

in the Year of the Earth Boar

KONSEPBOOKS
ASTROLOGY . FENG SHUI . INSPIRATIONS

FORTUNE & FENG SHUI 2019 TIGER

by Lillian Too and Jennifer Too

Published by KONSEP LAGENDA SDN BHD (223 855)
Kuala Lumpur 59100 Malaysia

For more Konsep books, go to www.lillian-too.com or www.wofs.com
To report errors, please send a note to errors@konsepbooks.com
For general feedback, email feedback@konsepbooks.com

ISBN 978-967-329-250-9
Published in Malaysia, September 2018

Tiger 2019

Birth Year	Western Calendar Dates	Age	Kua Number Males	Kua Number Females
Fire Tiger	13 Feb 1926 - 1 Feb 1927	93	2 West Group	4 East Group
Earth Tiger	31 Jan 1938 - 18 Feb 1939	81	8 West Group	7 West Group
Metal Tiger	17 Feb 1950 - 5 Feb 1951	69	5/2 West Group	1 East Group
Water Tiger	5 Feb 1962 - 24 Jan 1963	57	2 West Group	4 East Group
Wood Tiger	23 Jan 1974 - 10 Feb 1975	45	8 West Group	7 West Group
Fire Tiger	9 Feb 1986 - 28 Jan 1987	33	5/2 West Group	1 East Group
Earth Tiger	28 Jan 1998 - 15 Feb 1999	21	2 West Group	4 East Group
Metal Tiger	14 Feb 2010 - 2 Feb 2011	9	8 West Group	7 West Group

Contents

Contents

CHAPTER FOUR

Introduction

Outlook for Year 2019

Success & Stability in the Yin Earth Boar Year

This year, the world will experience much noticeable improvement in the stability of relations between countries. There will be greater harmony in 2019, the year of the Earth Boar, first of the two Water signs, so we shall experience greater incidences of success amidst a peaceful environment, as well as greater prosperity for many.

For those with the ambition and determination to aim high, this will be a year of outstanding opportunities to make the leap into new levels of attainment. The challenge of 2019 is whether or not you are clear-minded about what you want. For those who are, this can be a *break-out* year, as opportunities will not be hard to find.

> Success in attaining higher ranks of authority and power are there for those with ambition; and there is also WEALTH luck in abundance!

Creativity of ideas emerge and inspiration comes from many different sources. Many will find they can rely on their spouse or partners for needed resources to fulfill a dream or to take advantage of an opportunity.

DOMINANCE OF YOUTH

Wealth is found from the younger generation, as it seems that the source of affluence emanates from the youth of today. It will be the younger generation that will surprise the world with their fresh and original ideas. Many feel empowered by the Digital Age, and many will fast-track their paths to success taking this route. We see also the rise of automated intelligence brought about by the Artificial Intelligence revolution.

Many opt to go their own way, turning their backs on the traditional routes to attaining success. Parents must be prepared for the unconventionality of ideas inside the heads of the younger generation.

Our advice is to go with the flow, as this is the year of a Water sign, and water needs to flow. When water is allowed to flow, even the hardest obstacles can be overcome.

GOOD BALANCE OF ELEMENTS

This is a year when there is incredibly good balance of elements in the Paht Chee chart of the year. There is no shortage of any element in 2019, so it is generally a good year. It can be viewed as a time to reap gains from projects started in past years, but it is also a good time to begin new ventures which you may have been mulling over. This is because 2019 is a year when there is a good supply of wealth luck.

In terms of your career or business, you can consolidate or you can go on to seek out larger goals. There is *growth energy*, as the self-element for the year is Water in the chart sitting on Yang Metal. You can go after something grander if this

FOUR PILLARS

HOUR	DAY	MONTH	YEAR
丙 *Yang Fire*	壬 *Yang Water*	丙 *Yang Fire*	己 *Yin Earth*
丙 午 *Yang Fire Horse*	庚 申 *Yang Metal Monkey*	甲 寅 *Yang Wood Tiger*	癸 亥 *Yin Water Boar*

The 2019 Paht Chee chart is well-balanced with no missing elements, indicating a generally good year ahead.

is what you have always dreamt of. This is a good year to THINK BIG as the DAY Pillar of the year's chart is productive, with Metal producing Water, indicating that the resources of the year can be put to good use. It benefits to have a broad-based vision, to have ambition and to have the courage to take action.

Have faith in yourself. Shore up your confidence levels and take heart that luck is good this year for those getting into new careers or setting up new ventures. It favours those who are brave and those who dare to take risks. Those who are not, set limits on themselves. This is a year that favours those who know what they want, even if it is just the vague notion that they want to get richer, live longer or just be more adventurous and see the world.

The key to success this year comes from taking action and taking the short-term view. Let the long term take care of itself!

Always remember that this is a year when Water must flow, and Earth will show you when to slow down!

BOOSTING WEALTH LUCK

Note that this year's Boar brings lots of wealth luck. There is wonderful new wealth to be created. Success is mainly made by the young generation and ripens at the end of the year. The fourth quarter of 2019 is a time when there will be great wealth luck created. This is clearly indicated in the Paht Chee chart of 2019. Note that the element for wealth luck in 2019 is FIRE, so generate Fire energy to reflect

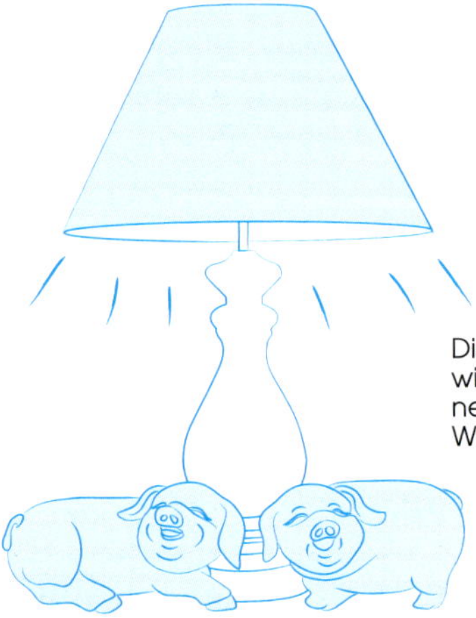

Display a pair of Boar with light source nearby to activate Wealth Luck this year.

this cosmic indication. This is the way to attract wealth luck this year. Turn on the lights in your home and keep the candles on your altar burning through the day and most of the night!

And note that while the Boar year brings wealth luck, when there is the presence of a pair of Boar, they bring the prosperity luck of plenty of Water. But also let there be the element of Fire energy nearby to actualize the cosmic forces that are needed to jumpstart the flowing in of wealth luck.

POWER & RECOGNITION

The Boar Year in 2019 is a YIN year, when the element of EARTH is the heavenly stem bringing power and recognition. This means that those wishing to gain additional power should connect strongly with the element of Earth.

This can be achieved by symbolically having **large porcelain vases** in the home, especially to the left or right side corner of the entrance. This will symbolically capture the Earth energies that enter into the home. When these corners also correspond to the SW or NE, it is even better, as these are the Earth element corners of your home.

Large porcelain vases capture Earth energy for the home. In 2019, Earth element energy brings power and recognition luck.

Note that the **symbol of the Vase** is an eternal receptacle for wealth and happiness in abundance. The vase also brings plentiful progeny luck, and all the older families of Hong Kong and China who follow tradition always display at least one pair if not more of large ceramic or porcelain vases in their homes. The larger the vase, the bigger the prosperity luck you will amass, but always, the size must be in proportion to the size of the living area of your home. Even a single VASE spells good fortune!

Displaying vases in the home is extremely lucky. They act as receptacles for wealth.

The Earth element this year symbolizes the attainment of power; and wanting to enhance your Power Luck means wanting to enjoy greater authority in whatever work you are engaged in, wanting to gain a higher rank in your organization, or in getting a well-deserved promotion. It is about connecting strongly with your inner silent ambitions. Those of you moving into a new job are sure to benefit from activating the Earth element near you, either in the Earth corners of your desks or work areas or in your homes.

EARTH element enhancers mean anything that comes from the earth. These can be porcelain decorative items such as ceramic plates, bowls and vases, crystals of various kinds or gemstones in different colours. The most potent are the wish-granting jewels and large earth-coloured crystal balls inscribed with auspicious mantras or sutras. These are symbolic enhancers that take on plenty of manifesting energy from you when you focus your intentions onto them.

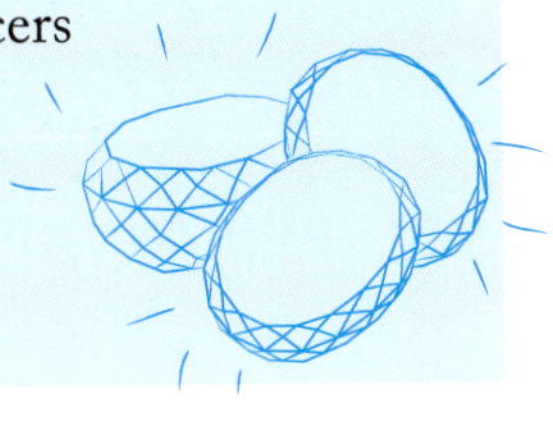

DO NOT BE HASTY!

In the year of the Boar that is ruled by the heavenly stem of Earth, patience yields favourable outcomes, so whatever situation faces you this coming year, you must give yourself time to think before making important decisions.

Ponder and consider and **do not rush into taking action**! This influence of the Earth element is what will empower you, bringing authenticity and greater chance for success as a result of your actions. Symbolically speaking, having the presence of the Earth element near you will steer you the way that brings you big success. You will make good decisions!

These are decisions that have to do with changing jobs, relocating to a new country or city, moving to a new house, or starting a new venture that requires a change of pace or new environment. Even in matters of the heart, it benefits not to be hasty.

The Earth element allows you to stay grounded, even as it empowers you.

The key word for 2019 is "PROSPERITY"

The year is dominated by the star of 8, which is also the number that dominates the current period. The number 8 is a strong number that stands for prosperity and good fortune. It is also supported by a very auspicious Paht Chee chart in this Earth Boar year, hence the year provides the kind of environment for the 8 to bring strong financial and economic growth. The number 8 is also an Earth number, so there is great power in the wealth luck it manifests.

As always, the year benefits those who have strong life force helping you. This year, the Wood signs - the TIGER and RABBIT - are blessed with excellent life force, while the Earth signs - OX, DOG, DRAGON and SHEEP - enjoy very good levels of life force. These six signs will find they have great clarity of vision to truly get the most from the year. Their actions can yield good results, but success comes only to those who enhance their *lung ta*.

Whether or not your life force is strong, you need to strengthen your **personal windhorse**. In 2019, success luck in terms of personal *lung ta* strength is lacking, and indeed, only one sign, that of the Ox, has a Windhorse strong enough to match its life force this year. All other animals benefit from carrying the **Life Force Enhancing Talisman.**

MUST STRENGTHEN WINDHORSE in 2019

Everyone needs help to get their cosmic success luck strengthened, and this year, only the trinity of allies that comprise the OX, ROOSTER and SNAKE are the three signs that enjoy very good Windhorse luck. The other nine signs have either Neutral or Low levels of *lung ta*. This is not surprising, as the elements of the year are Earth and Water.

This year, only the Ox, Rooster & Snake enjoy excellent Windhorse levels - i.e. propensity to succeed. All other signs really need the Windhorse this year.

Everyone needs the Windhorse in 2019, but especially the TIGER, whose *lung ta* levels are not good this year.

To enjoy the luck of the Windhorse, it is beneficial to display a large image of the Windhorse that flies into the skies bringing success luck from the cosmic heavens.

The Windhorse is the great success steed of the mighty King Gesar. For the year 2019, having the presence of this mighty Protector Warrior God continues to be beneficial, but it is also beneficial to display his mighty Windhorse to ensure that whatever new project you undertake will meet with success for you, or at least that your new venture will not fail.

PAHT CHEE CHART OF 2019

The *Four Pillars Chart* that rules this Earth Boar year of 2019 is extremely well-balanced, indicating plenty of WEALTH luck as well as plenty of cooperation amongst countries and companies. It is surprisingly less competitive than previous years, and this is probably due to the presence of all five elements, thereby bringing stability and a wish for peace through the year.

FOUR PILLARS

HOUR	DAY	MONTH	YEAR
丙 *Yang Fire*	壬 *Yang Water*	丙 *Yang Fire*	己 *Yin Earth*
丙午 *Yang Fire Horse*	庚申 *Yang Metal Monkey*	甲寅 *Yang Wood Tiger*	癸亥 *Yin Water Boar*

The year is dominated by the FIRE element, which in 2019 signifies WEALTH luck. There is therefore a great deal of new wealth luck that can get created this year, not surprising as the animal sign this year is the Boar, which brings good prosperity luck associated with WATER. Together, the two elements are very strong, and there will be the luck of power, order and authority. Hence the ambience of the year favours economic growth.

Wealth creation in 2019 is led by the younger generation, and this appears to be the trend of the past decade. We are well into the digital age, which is led by the creativity and mind power of the young. This trend continues into 2019.

The Paht Chee chart also reveals that the element of WATER in 2019 stands for friendships and good cooperation. The creation of wealth and financial success is thus strengthened with many new strategic alliances getting forged this year. There are no missing elements in the chart, and the dominance of FIRE and WATER is complemented by the presence of a single METAL, which stands for resources, a single EARTH which stands for power and a single element of WOOD which stands for creativity and mental capability.

All five elements are present, and they combine harmoniously to increase wealth creation this year. This indicates that it will be a good year.

WEALTH LUCK IN 2019

Those wanting to participate in the overflowing financial and prosperity luck of the year should wear red and keep their homes well lit. The best is to display **Treasure Chest Dharani** and shine a bright light over it. Put it near you if possible in the South corner. This symbolizes powerful Fire element energy bringing great good fortune.

Place on your table in the center of your home, or in the South sector of your home. Here, the Fire energy dispels the bad energies brought by the #3 star, which is in the South this year. Here the # 3 star is very powerful and needs to be subdued with Fire energy.

Placing the Treasure Chest Dharani will not only welcome wealth luck into the home, but will also suppress the troublesome star of 3, which flies there in 2019.

The Treasure Chest Dharani makes a fabulous wealth energiser for 2019. Place in the South or center of the home.

You can also invite into your home **White Dzambhala and Four Daikinis** if you have not already done so. The four offering goddesses, known as Dakinis in Tibetan Buddhism, come from the Jewel family, the Vajra family, the Lotus family and the Action family, and with these Dakinis in your home, wealth luck gets energized.

The five Dzambhalas are the wealth-bringing Buddhas.

Or you can invite one or ***all five Dzambhalas***. These are wealth-bringing Buddhas who each signify one of the five elements. It is excellent having them in the home when the energy all five elements are present in the year's Paht Chee chart. These are the White, Yellow, Black, Red and Green Dzambhalas.

In addition, you can invite the Lord of all the Wealth Gods, who is also one of the Four Great Kings. This is a great year to welcome all four of these Great Kings into your home.

Here, we are entering into the practice of *Spiritual Feng Shui* where we invoke the help of the celestial cosmic Gods of Wealth. In different traditions, Wealth Gods have different names and wear different attire, but in the cosmic realms, all the Wealth Gods respect and honour each other. A home that displays the images of these Wealth Gods invokes their powerful blessings.

SUCCESS LUCK IN 2019

This category of luck is not as easily forthcoming in the Year of the Boar. Readers wishing to strengthen their career luck or wanting to gain sufficient recognition to earn promotion through the course of the year will require the assistance of the all-powerful **King Gesar riding the Windhorse** or by having the **Banner of Victory** prominently displayed near their work space. Hanging the **Windhorse flag** on a high point of the home will also strengthen success luck.

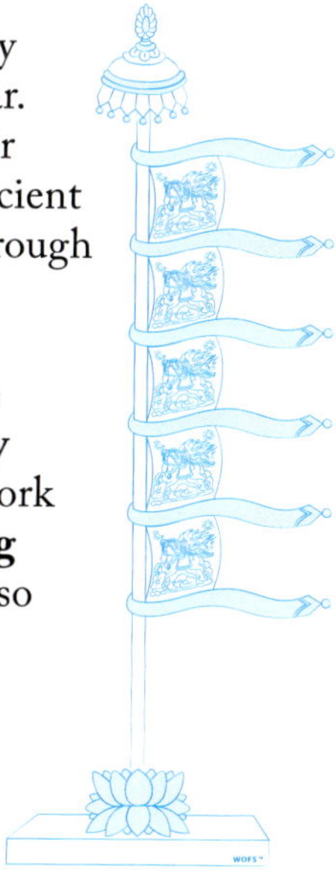

The Banner of Victory activates the kind of luck that lets you come out on top in any "competitive" situation

OBSERVATIONS OF THE 2019 CHART

Firstly, the Paht Chee chart shows an excellent balance and composition of elements that indicate abundance brought by the presence of all five elements with FIRE dominating. The strongest element is Fire, and there are THREE of this element. The great significance of this is that **Fire represents wealth luck** in 2019. For sure, there is the promise of wonderful economic growth for the world, and money-making will be direct and plentiful.

FOUR PILLARS

HOUR	DAY	MONTH	YEAR
丙 *Yang Fire*	壬 *Yang Water*	丙 *Yang Fire*	己 *Yin Earth*
丙午 *Yang Fire Horse*	庚申 *Yang Metal Monkey*	甲寅 *Yang Wood Tiger*	癸亥 *Yin Water Boar*

The 2019 Paht Chee chart is dominated by Fire, which represents WEALTH luck this year.

The New Year will see financial stability and the creation of NEW wealth. The element of Fire is present through the first, second and fourth quarters of the year, so money-making luck is spread out through the seasons of the year.

The presence of two showings of the WOOD element (one direct and one hidden) indicates there is both common sense and creativity. The overall mood of the year rewards smart people, and common sense prevails. This means that good judgement will override emotion-based actions. There will be good decisions made through the year, as WOOD also suggests good growth. This implies that in 2019, everyone can benefit from taking a reasonable approach. It is not a year to be foolhardy, emotional or impulsive.

There are no missing elements this year, so the presence of one each of the remaining elements of METAL, WATER and EARTH completes the basket of elements. There is also a plentiful supply of **hidden elements**, so there are no cosmic shortages during the year. This is good news as it indicates that all the factors necessary for there to be general good luck are present.

There are three elements of hidden EARTH, which suggests decisiveness and good authority luck through the year. There is no evidence of the "wild cards" present in previous years, making the world a generally safer place – less natural disasters, less accidents and less humankind violence.

THREE YANG & ONE YIN PILLAR

Second, there are three ***yang pillars*** and one ***yin pillar***. This indicates greater activity this year, as the yin and yang cosmic balance shows the yang energies dominating. It is only the YEAR Pillar that is YIN, so the strength of the yang pillars are dominant.

FOUR PILLARS

HOUR	DAY	MONTH	YEAR
丙 *Yang Fire*	壬 *Yang Water*	丙 *Yang Fire*	己 *Yin Earth*
丙午 *Yang Fire Horse*	庚申 *Yang Metal Monkey*	甲寅 *Yang Wood Tiger*	癸亥 *Yin Water Boar*

3 of the 4 pillars are YANG, indicating greater activity this year.

Activity and a vigourous dynamic suggests that the movers and shakers of the world are more inclined to take logic-derived risks.

We see the tremendous rise of artificial intelligence and this means that increasingly, mankind will turn to the quantum way of making decisions, with machines doing the probability calculations for us. There will be less input of emotions in decision making. This is not necessarily a good thing, but how it affects the world is not easy to predict.

Generally, it will be the younger generation who will be far more comfortable with the new style scenario! The chart shows the younger generation getting richer too!

TWO IMPORTANT AFFINITIES

Third, the four Earthly Branches of the Pillars show two important affinities with the Year Pillar of BOAR forming a secret friendship with the Month Pillar of TIGER. This means there is respect for elders. The younger generation will not ignore the counsel of their parents. The Tiger is also an ally of the Horse, which appears in the

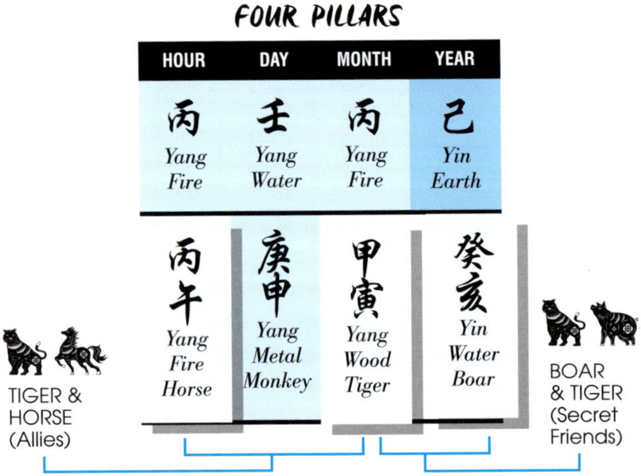

Hour Pillar, and this suggests that the generations have good relations. There is room for prosperity to manifest within families, as father and son, bosses and subordinates work well together. This is the secret strength of 2019.

The two animal signs Boar and Tiger are extremely harmonious, and together, these two signs bring a good mix of diplomacy and forward thinking that generate good working relationships. The Boar has a gentle disposition, while the Tiger is family oriented;

this is a combination that indicates harmonious cooperation. More importantly, the Boar brings the Water energy of prosperity and this is represented by a pair of happy Boars entering the home bringing Water. This is a popular Chinese saying and in 2019, it is extremely beneficial to display **a pair of Boar**, as this signifies an Abundance of Water being brought into the home.

The major conflict of Earthly branches is the **Monkey/Tiger clash**. This may cause toxic relations to flare up between young couples and their parents. Should you observe increased disagreements in households where parents live with their married children, the way to overcome this clash is to display the **image of a pair of Boar**. This simple astrological remedy will appease the older folk. Here, the Boar is the secret friend of the Tiger, and the presence of a pair of Boar will smooth out all conflict energies.

A pair of "happy Boar bringing water" will improve relations within the household especially between the different generations.

FOUR ELEMENTS CROSS

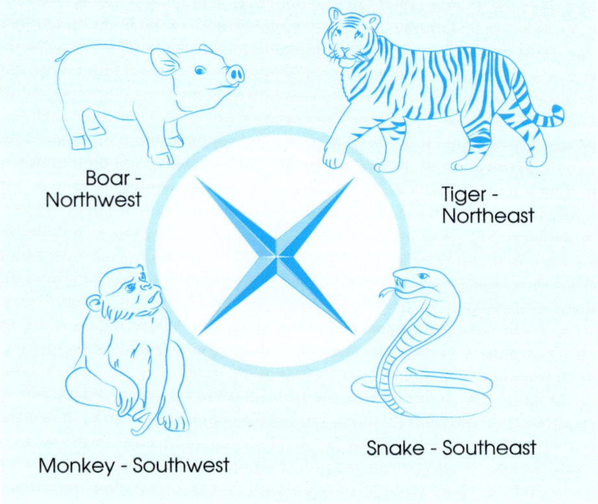

Better yet, you can bring into your home the **image of the Snake** to create the **Four Elements Cross** comprising the **Tiger/Monkey/ Boar/Snake.** This cross is made up of two sets of "clashing" animal signs, and it transforms something toxic into something powerful. Displaying the **4 Elements Cross Mirror** in the home

effectively nullifies this conflict in the year's Paht Chee as well as activates for superior wealth luck for the whole family.

STRONG EMPOWERMENT LUCK

Fourth, there is strong *recognition and empowerment luck* signified by the element of ***EARTH*** present in the main chart with also three hidden EARTH. The authority of laws and superiors is recognized, and good sense will always triumph over extremists and troublemakers in this Year of the Boar, which continues the trend towards a maturing Period of 8. It does indicate that the world is turning towards a period of reconciliation and turning away from using violence. Hopefully, this will cause nations hostile to each other to turn to negotiating peace rather than resorting to war!

3 PROMISING STARS

Fifth, the year has three promising good stars and one unlucky star! The auspicious stars in the year's Four Pillars chart are the *Star of Prospects*, the *Scholastic Brilliance Star* and the *Diplomat Star*.

Star of Prospects

Star of Scholastic Brilliance

Diplomat Star

These stars bring satisfaction and happiness, but they are stars that manifest when there is personal effort made to see them bring the light of good luck one's way. To fully enjoy their impact, it is necessary to stimulate and activate them.

The Chinese always look to activate the astrological "stars" of the Paht Chee and in this regard, we look on readings differently from the way Western Astrology regards them. To the Chinese, life's fortunes are always influenced by the input of yang energy. All auspicious indications thus need to be *activated* – infused with yang chi to manifest good fortune – and it is this that adds the dimension of self effort.

Good fortune luck needs to be activated in order to manifest good fortune.

FAVOURABLE STARS OF 2019

1. STAR OF SCHOLASTIC BRILLIANCE

FOUR PILLARS

HOUR	DAY	MONTH	YEAR
丙 *Yang Fire*	壬 *Yang Water*	丙 *Yang Fire*	己 *Yin Earth*
丙午 *Yang Fire Horse*	庚申 *Yang Metal Monkey*	甲寅 *Yang Wood Tiger*	癸亥 *Yin Water Boar*

The Star of Scholastic Brilliance in 2019's chart brings success luck to those pursuing knowledge and scholarships.

This star is shining auspiciously this year, bringing special good fortune to those who strive for academic success. It is brought by the combination of *YANG WATER in the Day Pillar with the TIGER of the Month Pillar*, hence this is a happy Tiger who spends time contemplating and studying and bringing good fortune related to academic success. Here, the higher one aims for success, the more spectacular can be the level of attainment achieved.

This star indicates that the year will see serious thinkers and academicians gaining recognition. Hard work and diligence will be recognized and smart people will gain renown. The pursuit of excellence will enjoy new interest, and clever people gain the respect and recognition of powerful people.

It is a year when academic excellence is given importance. This star means great esteem is given to learning, and those who achieve good results in public examinations or who graduate with high honours can aspire to higher paying jobs.

The way to magnify this star that brings recognition of educational success is to introduce the **Sage** sitting on a happy and complacent Tiger. Here, not only does this placement bring excellent scholastic success, the Tiger also brings financial assistance of some kind, such as a scholarship or sponsorship from a benefactor.

The Sage on a Tiger brings scholastic excellence to students and financial assistance from a benefactor.

2. STAR OF PROSPECTS brings WEALTH luck

This is a very favourable star. It appears in the 2019 chart because the heavenly stem of the *Day Pillar is Yang Water*, and this combines with the *Yin Water Boar of the Year Pillar* bringing great wealth luck. It is favourable for those for whom the element of Water is favourable. To know this, you need to know your personal Paht Chee chart. If your chart has **Weak Wood** in the heavenly stem of your Day Pillar, then this *Star of Prospects* is sure to bring you NEW wealth this year!

FOUR PILLARS

HOUR	DAY	MONTH	YEAR
丙 *Yang Fire*	壬 *Yang Water*	丙 *Yang Fire*	己 *Yin Earth*
丙 午 *Yang Fire Horse*	庚 申 *Yang Metal Monkey*	甲 寅 *Yang Wood Tiger*	癸 亥 *Yin Water Boar*

The Star of Prospects brings wealth luck to those for whom the Water element is favourable.

This star also benefits those born in the years of the **RABBIT** and **TIGER**, both of which are WOOD signs.

Those whose charts are described as above are in harmony with this star; you will then possess a powerful **competitive edge** in any field of endeavour you carve out for yourself. Generally, the presence of this star brings determination and staying power, as well as the passion to succeed. The feeling is that there is nothing that cannot be achieved.

There is hence the grit and the willpower to work diligently. Many people will be fired up by the ambition to succeed and strive to achieve new aspirations. The presence of this star also indicates that this is a year when those in need of capital will find it easy to get financial support – unless the element of Water is bad for them based on their charts. Otherwise, this is a very favourable star this year.

You can amplify the benefits of this star if you can activate it to manifest its favourable energies. Do this by placing a beautiful tree of prosperity that benefits from the Water energy which brings you this star.

FENG SHUI ENHANCER: Display the **Music Tree** in the sectors of the Rabbit or Tiger, which are East or NE. Let the tinkling sounds of the music play regularly to attract wonderful prospective energies your way. Doing so will attract wealth luck, bringing good prospects and opportunities of all kinds.

3. STAR OF THE DIPLOMAT

The presence of this powerful star in the 2019 chart brings good fortune that arises from there being a peaceful environment prevailing through the year. There is less chance of misunderstandings arising from miscommunication or anger energies. It is a year when quarrels get resolved and tempers are kept in check. The air is filled with reconciliation energies. Hostility situations are less likely. The year will thus have fewer legal problems arising. Work environments are also less stressful.

The best way to activate the Diplomat Star is to energize the NW of the home with the presence of the Boar image.

Activate the NW sector with a water feature with a pair of Boar nearby.

Here a **water feature** with a **family of Boar**, or with a pair of Boar is an excellent symbolic energizer for 2019. Placed in the NW of the office, it ensures harmony in the office, and placed in the NW of the home, it brings great diplomacy into homes. Siblings get along better and spouses will see the good side of each other.

ONE UNFORTUNATE STAR

SQUANDERING STAR

2019 is a year that offers great potential for those keen on making the most of themselves, but do take note also that there is one strong unfortunate star, which signals the danger of succumbing to one's own negativities. Giving in to feelings of anger, jealousy, loneliness or having thoughts of revenge can lead to great misfortune, even when it may seem that you are having the upper hand.

Note that there is the presence of the *Squandering Star* in the chart, which can prove to be very unlucky indeed. This star triggers all the hidden negativities in people, magnifying their feelings of unhappiness or pent up anger. This can cause those having such negative attitudes to take action that leads to wasting away the year's good fortune energies. This can lead to misfortune.

FOUR PILLARS

HOUR	DAY	MONTH	YEAR
丙 *Yang Fire*	壬 *Yang Water*	丙 *Yang Fire*	己 *Yin Earth*
丙午 *Yang Fire Horse*	庚申 *Yang Metal Monkey*	甲寅 *Yang Wood Tiger*	癸亥 *Yin Water Boar*

The Squandering Star can cause one to waste good fortune opportunities that come your way.

Thus, it is important NOT to give in to negative thoughts, and instead, work at bringing out your good side!

The SQUANDERING STAR is a very unfortunate star as it means there is also the possibility that much of the good fortune of the year can get squandered i.e. wasted away by those unable to appreciate their own good fortune. In the chart, this star is caused by the *MONKEY of the Day Pillar* clashing directly with the *TIGER of the Month Pillar*. The clash of these two animal signs can be severe and it affects the luck of all those born or married to anyone born in the year of the Monkey.

FENG SHUI AMULET: The way to overcome this unfortunate star is to carry the **Boar amulet**! Overcome the affliction brought by this star by using the "secret friend" cure signified by the Boar and Tiger being astrological secret friends. Since this is an astrological affliction, what you need is an astrological cure! So wear this amulet or keep it near you to ensure you do not suffer the effects of the *Squandering Star!*

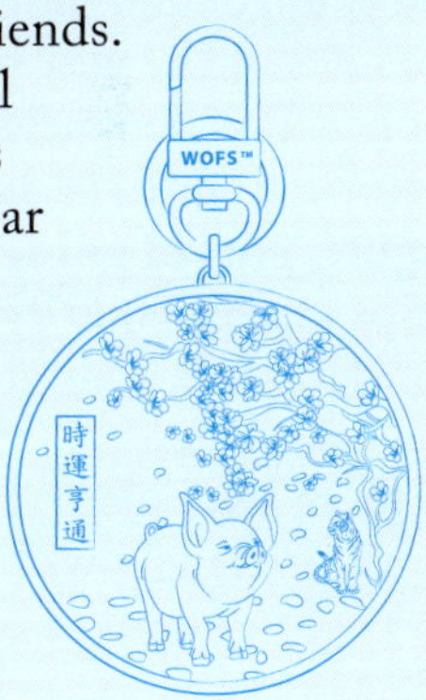

Carry the Boar Amulet to overcome the Squandering Star of the year.

DIRECT & INDIRECT WEALTH LUCK

There are many of positive wealth luck indications this year and there is both *direct* and *indirect* wealth. Prosperity can be created or manifested by the younger and older generations, so the annual energies of the year strongly favour making money. It is beneficial to place symbols of good fortune around the home – these include **coins, ingots, pots of gold, treasure chests, wealth ships** and **prosperity vases** and so forth.

In a year when wealth luck is plentiful, the more of these symbols you have around the home, the more amazingly will wealth luck manifest for you.

WEALTH ENERGISER:
The best is to create a large **Wealth Vessel** in which you place auspicious golden ingots, gold bars, even real coins and cash notes in different currencies!

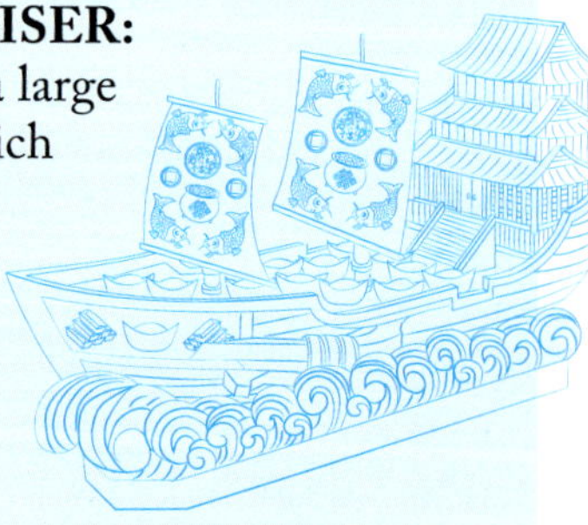

ELEMENT LUCK OF THE TIGER

Those amongst you having the best WEALTH LUCK in 2019 are the **69 year old Metal Tiger** and also the **45 year old Wood Tiger**. The Tiger sign has a special association with the Wealth Gods of many different countries of Asia.

This is a sign who enjoys excellent life force and spirit essence in 2019, and only one other sign enjoys this indication. This means that you are very well placed to benefit from the extraordinary wealth luck of the year.

AMULET: To ensure you do not lose out on this wealth bonanza, carry the **Wealth Fox Amulet**. This amulet ensures you can turn all money-making opportunities into successes for yourself.

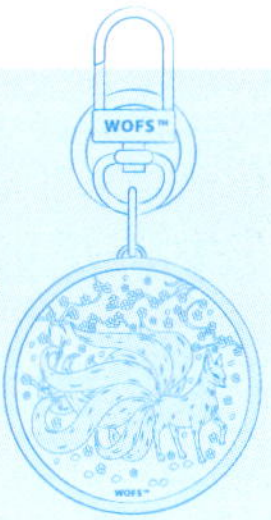

The Chinese always associate Tiger sign with their Prosperity Gods, and especially with Tsai Shen Yeh, the powerful wealth deity who brings abundance to households who invite his image into their home. The Hindu Wealth Goddess Lakshmi and their Earth Goddess Durga also sit

The Chinese always associate the Tiger with Prosperity Gods, and many of their Wealth Deities are depicted sitting on Tigers.

on Tigers, as do many of their other Goddesses of fertility and abundance.

In 2019, the Tiger is in great harmony with the year, as the Boar is its secret friend, so there is synchronicity of energy that will benefit you. The Tiger's personal *lung ta* is very afflicted this year, so wear the **Windhorse Strengthening Amulet** at all times. The good luck for you is that in 2019, your intrinsic WOOD energy will bring you the luck of creativity and intelligence.

IMPORTANT ENHANCERS FOR THE YEAR

WEALTH ACTIVATING AMULET

For activation of wealth luck, everyone should wear or carry inside your handbag the powerful **Wealth Activation Amulet** specially made to light up the fire of wealth. This will ensure that the year's prolific wealth luck will manifest directly for you.

This amulet may be worn or displayed inside the home to ensure the whole family benefits from its powerful wish-activating mantra placed within the amulet to trigger the prosperity aura necessary so you can participate in the year's wealth-creating energies.

Wealth Activation Amulet

WEALTH WALLET

It is always beneficial to get a NEW wealth wallet to generate fresh wealth-creating ideas for the new year. And then to ensure a continuity of good fortune, you should always transfer some old money into the new wallet. To welcome fresh prosperity, you must also place new money into the wallet.

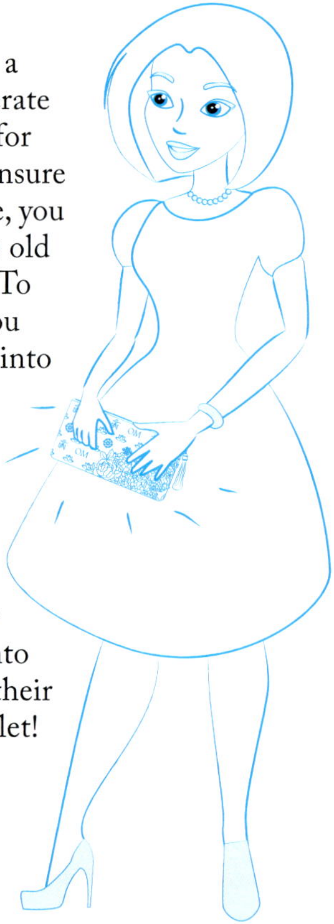

If someone "gives" you lucky money during the 15 days of the Lunar New Year, or if you have money given to you from a wealthy man's pocket, placing this into your wallet is sure to bring their wealth energy into your wallet!

THE POWER OF RED IN 2019

In 2019, the FIRE element is the most important element, as this is the year's WEALTH element. Red is hence the best colour to wear if you want to attract wealth luck towards you. Make sure to always wear or carry some red – as a scarf, carrying a wallet or bag, or by wearing bright red lipstick. All this will strengthen your wealth luck for the year. Check out our range of predominantly **red scarves and wallets**.

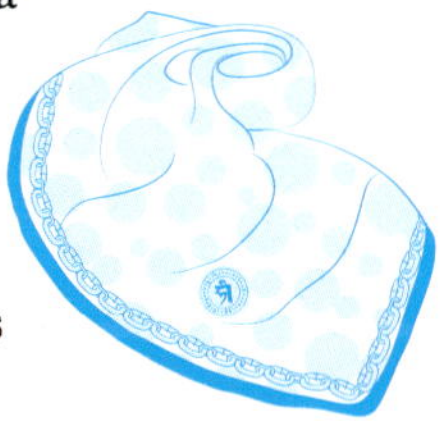

For the first time, we are creating an auspicious **Red Candle** for wealth luck for the year, so do make sure you light up a red candle at least once a week to generate wealth luck inside your home. Let the candle burn through the day, as this ensures the presence of yang chi.

WEALTH VASES FOR THE YEAR

In 2019, everyone benefits from displaying special bespoke vases that attract wealth luck for each of the four groupings of allies. Each of the four vases carry auspicious designs. Each also contains mantras, as well as representations of the five elements.

Treasure Vase

Action Vase

Great Increasing Vase

Luminious Vase

For those born in Dog, Tiger and Horse years:
It is especially beneficial to display the **ACTION VASE** which contains the wish-granting mantra of Red Tara folded within!

For those born in Rabbit, Boar and Sheep years:
You should have the **LUMINIOUS VASE** with symbols of the excellent Stack of Auspiciousness sutra rolled within. This vase also contains the special Dharanis of Green Tara.

Those born in Rooster, Snake, Ox years:
These animal signs benefit greatly from displaying the **GREAT INCREASING VASE**. This vase contains the sacred sutra of the "Increasing Energy" of Yellow Tara folded within.

Those born in Monkey, Rat and Dragon years:
It is especially beneficial to display the **TREASURE VASE** which contains the symbols and wish-granting mantras of Black Tara folded within.

Vases bring blessing nectar that attract prosperity and good fortune. The Tara Goddesses always carry vases and Vasudhara, being the Goddess of Abundance, sprinkles prosperity blessings to households that display her image.

These are extremely powerful sacred items that are especially suitable for 2019 – a year with plenty of wealth luck. Vases have always been an auspicious symbol that signifies a state of riches. Vases are repositories of good fortune. All the Taras - the incredible Goddesses who liberate all from poverty in all its manifestations – carry vases that contain their special nectar blessings.

When the vases contain Tara's powerful mantras, seed syllables and dharanis - and are placed within home, on altars, on cabinet tops and near the dining area - they radiate wealth blessings to all the members of the household.

Managing your feng shui and astrological luck for the year keeps getting easier each year, as most everything you need to know and do are contained in these little books, which summarise all the up-to-date information you need for you to enjoy *good timing* and *excellent placement feng shui*.

These books give clarity to the way you make decisions for the year. You can also enjoy better confidence when scheduling the timing for taking action or for staying calm in the midst of chaos. When you go through the year, knowing when and how obstacles and afflictions can strike will improve your chances of enjoying success.

When the timing of your actions is in sync with the feng shui winds of the year, and also with your own astrological updates, then the probability of you getting the outcomes according to your wishes is increased. The vital importance of timing is something high achievers in any field are always aware of. Almost all who attain success acknowledge that good timing plays the most crucial role in their ongoing success. Hence it is always necessary to take note of the annual and monthly changes of energy, so you can cope successfully with the changing nature of luck.

Staying up to date on your astrological outlook helps you get your timing right.

We give weight to the impact of the Feng Shui Chart of each New Year because this reveals the feng shui afflictions sector by sector. Identifying the afflicted sectors enable these afflictions to get treated with suitable remedies and with specially-designed element cures.

These remedies can be extremely beneficial as they are designed to suppress all bad, all excessively yin and all harmful energies. Our remedies and cures possess exciting authenticity as we are careful that the symbolic signs and the mantras embedded are applied with care and respect. We are strict on design and quality control because we know how important the energy "attached" to feng shui cures are. And it is this motivational power that gives our amulets much strength.

Likewise, the lucky aspects of the year's feng shui chart and astrological indications provide us with invaluable information to design our good fortune enhancers. The good sectors of 2019's chart, which is dominated by the auspicious number 8, must be activated with the correct placement of powerful symbols that bring specific types of good fortune.

THE ART OF PLACEMENT

This is probably the easiest way to attract good fortune your way. Place the correct auspicious enhancer into the right corners of your living room, foyer, dining area, bedroom and so forth. This is the crux of Symbolic Feng Shui, which has its roots in Flying Star feng shui – a compass-based formula which pays attention to the changing energies and the impact of lucky "numbers" as well as numbers that bring afflictions.

When auspicious sectors of rooms – either at home or in the office – are activated by specially-placed decorative items, the energy brought by the new year gets energized and then they bring amazing good fortune. From these ancient formulas come methods of feng shui that are so relevant for the modern age. We have been using this easy method of feng shui for so long, over three decades, that we are just so in awe of them.

But of course, it is not as easy as it seems, because behind the recommendations for the specific sectors of the rooms every year lie plenty of research and accurate design work. Creating the objects – the feng shui cures as well as the enhancers, talismans and amulets – requires careful planning. Due consideration must be given to the combinations of numbers, elements, directions and astrological signs and also the stars of the 24 Mountains and the ruling elements of the different pillars of luck that rule the year.

All of that is then put together and offered in the easiest way possible to you.

Our goal is to ensure your luck for the year gets immediately improved. We know that the popularity of our books, cures and enhancers, our amulets, talismans and wearables and our scarves and jewellery, stems from only one thing.

THEY WORK and they work very well!

Our cures and amulets are so effective for helping people avoid misfortune luck because we know how to pinpoint the exact nature of afflictions. Our beautiful enhancers work like magic because we place so much sacred energy into them. Our supplier factories in China, Hong Kong, Malaysia and elsewhere have just been incredible in observing all the rituals we teach them to observe when they make our sacred items.

As a result, these enhancers are so good at enhancing the lifestyles of those who display them. So the art of placement is easy. Read the feng shui energy pattern of 2019 and then place the cures and enhancers as recommended.

THE ENERGY MIX OF 2019

The Feng Shui Chart of 2019 is dominated by a supremely auspicious number 8, bringing auspicious luck for everyone this year. This means that all houses and all buildings - indeed all built up structures - have a powerful central core of lucky energy! This being also the Period of 8, this is an exceedingly strong number! Shown here then is the chart of the New Year.

Feng Shui Chart of 2019

The 2019 chart can be superimposed onto rooms of homes and offices alike. Use a compass to anchor the chart so that the compass directions of the chart are placed correctly to reflect the real direction/location of the layout plan of the house. Familiarize yourself with the numbers in each sector according to the chart so you know which sectors contain the lucky numbers, and which sectors house numbers that bring afflictions.

This way, you instantly know what the lucky and unlucky corners of rooms are. The chart has lucky number 8 in the center, so every room and every office benefits from this feature in 2019.

As you read about the eight sectors of each of the important rooms of your home or office, you will be able to identify which number dominates which corner of the room. You can do this for every room that is important to you, and this means the rooms where you spend the most amount of time.

You can systematically take notes of the energy pattern for the year. Use a reliable compass to identify the sectors of every room and then take note of the afflictions and the remedy needed as well as the good luck sectors and what enhancer you want to place in that corner. Auspicious enhancers must be placed to strengthen the lucky corners of 2019 and this will ensure the flow of good fortune gets attracted into the home. Likewise, the remedies must also be placed into the corners requiring these afflictions to be suppressed. This is the practice of *placement* in Time Dimension Feng Shui and this is what is needed for you to stay protected and safe. It also ensures you can maximize your personal luck as well as the luck of your home.

IDENTIFYING THE IMPORTANT SECTORS

THE CENTER has the lucky star 8

In 2019, the center of any room is vital and since we have seen that:

1. The center number is the magnificent 8.
2. The colour RED is very auspicious it being the WEALTH colour.
3. The center is ruled by the EARTH element.

The most important thing is that the center of your living room, and any other important room, such as the study, dining and even the bedroom should be activated by making sure all or at least one of the following is placed to energize the center sector.

- Have a ***bright warm light*** in the center of rooms. Change the bulb so you do not have white light. What is needed is yellow light. It is a great idea to keep this light turned on through the day and night so the 8 gets activated continuously.

- If you have a coffee table in your living room, place it in the center of the room and light a ***yellow or red candle*** here each day to activate the energy vibrations here. This will stimulate the number 8 into action.

- Place a ***bright red table lamp*** in the center to fire up the energy of 8 here as well as to generate wonderful wealth luck for the household.

- Activate the **Power of 8**, as this is the lucky number of the current period. It stands for current prosperity, so you can energize this by placing **8 wish-granting jewels, 8 solid ingots** and **8 sets of coins** tied with red thread inside a bowl here in the center.

- You can also place **a pair of Elephants** in the center of the living area, as this is considered extremely auspicious.

Place a pair of Elephants in the center of the living area.

To maximize the luck of #8 for the center, make an effort to fill the center of important rooms with as much *yang* chi as you can. This means creating activity, generating high noise level, and of course, keeping them well lit. When there is movement, sound and laughter, #8 comes to life, bringing good fortune and plenty of prosperity.

In the Constellation, the number 8 is a "man-made star" with two assistants – on the right and left. When it is strong, it brings wealth and great nobility. Since wealth luck is strong in 2019, it brings huge benefits to keep this number well-energized.

To maximise the luck of the #8 star in the center of the chart, keep the central hub of activity in your home full of yang energy - e.g. stereos, TVs, parties, kids playing, pets...

THE LUCKY SECTORS OF 2019

The lucky sectors with numbers 1 & 6

The lucky numbers of 1 and 6 span across the middle sector of the feng shui chart. Here, the compass directions are the EAST, the CENTER and the WEST of all rooms/homes/offices. These are the three sectors that benefit most from the

East, center and West are the three sectors enjoying the best luck in 2019, benefitting from the White Star numbers of 6, 8 and 1.

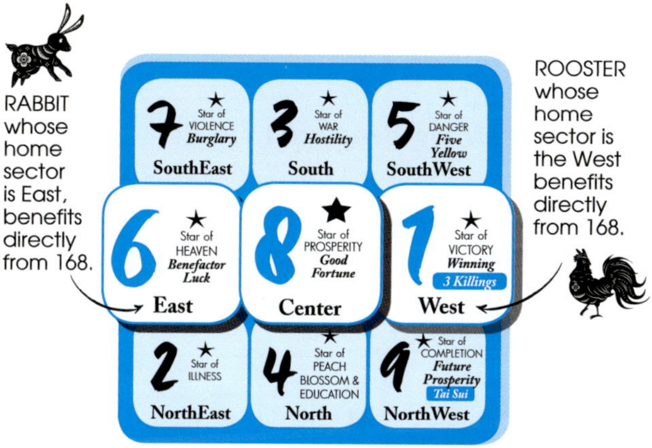

three white numbers 6, 8 and 1. These are the three lucky numbers of the Flying Star system, and just by displaying the numbers 168 on your car, or as part of your telephone or banking numbers, brings you good fortune.

In 2019, only two animal signs benefit directly from these lucky numbers, which are the **Rabbit** whose home sector is the East, and the **Rooster** whose home sector is the West. But all other signs can benefit from these lucky stars by ensuring these parts of the home are activated.

IN THE EAST
#6 HEAVENLY STAR
(bringing strong Benefactor Luck)

In 2019, the number 6 is in the EAST sector of rooms, and this number brings the *Benefactor Star of Heaven.* Here the feng shui energies have a celestial quality that benefits the Rabbit sign. This means that all those born under this sign and also those whose bedrooms or work rooms are located here will benefit from heaven's blessings. When this part of the room or home gets properly energized with good placements, the whole household will enjoy a smooth year. There are no major obstacles that cause projects to stall, nor will there be any failures to cause you unhappiness.

You can enhance the power of the number 6 by placing **auspicious windchimes** in the East, as the sound of *metal on metal* will activate the Metal number 6. Normally we would not recommend this for the East, as this is a Wood sector, but because the *Yearly Conflict Star* has flown here, the placement of the **Buddha's Foot Windchime** here will go a long way to suppressing the conflict energy while simultaneously enhancing the celestial 6.

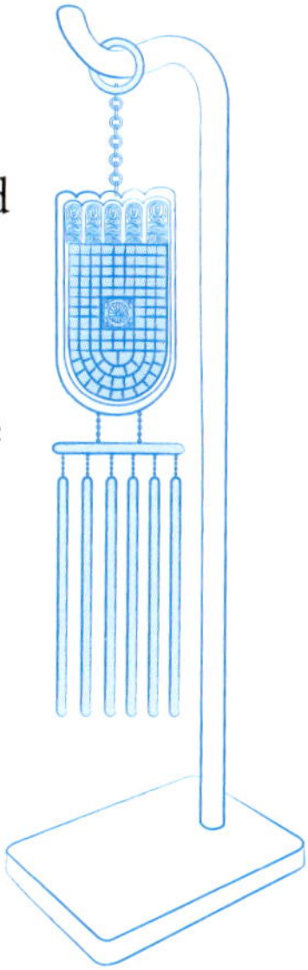

Place a Buddha's Foot Windchime in the East in 2019 to activate the Heavenly Star 6.

The East sector is also affected by the stars of the 24 Mountains, and in 2019, this corner of rooms suffers from facing the energies of the *Three Killings* sent its way by the Rabbit's astrological enemy the Rooster.

The Rabbit sign is also sitting on the *Star of Yearly Conflict*, and since this is a Wood sector, if you occupy this room or for those born in the year of the Rabbit, you must place **bright Fire energy** to suppress the conflict energies here.

IN THE WEST
#1 VICTORY STAR
(manifesting strong winning energies)

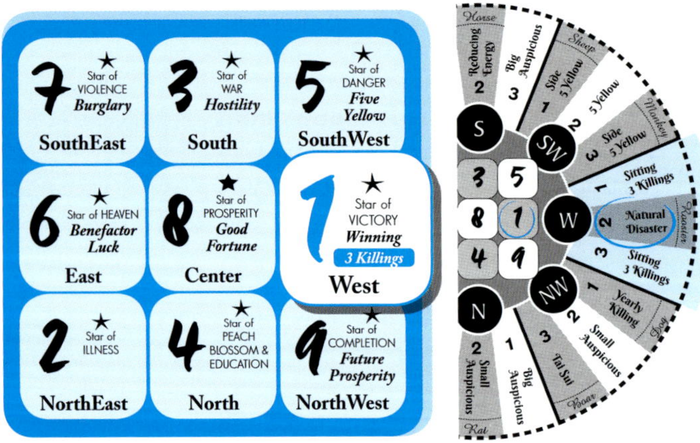

In 2019, the number 1 is in the WEST sector of rooms and homes, and this star number is the victory number. The white star 1 is associated with winning and attaining success over your competitors, so it generally brings victory luck to those enjoying its good influences.

In 2019, the Victory Star benefits residents whose bedrooms are located in the West; so if your bedroom is in this sector, you will enjoy a good amount of victory luck. The number 1 star is a white number, which also brings good fortune to those in leadership positions.

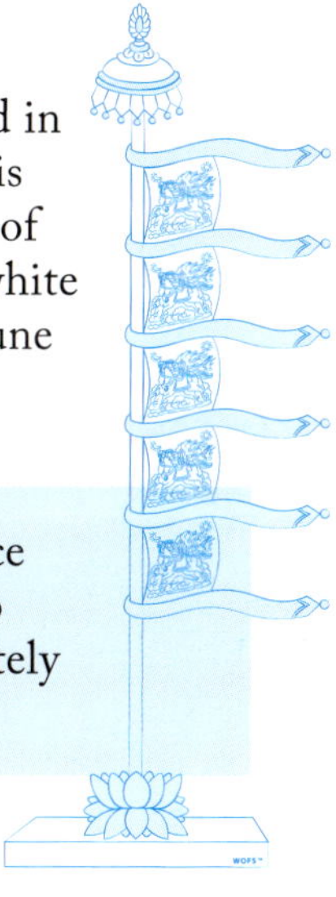

FENG SHUI ENHANCER: Place a **Banner of Victory** in the West to ensure that winning luck is adequately enhanced here

In 2019, the star number 1 benefits the Rooster sign, because the West is the Rooster sector of the home. Under normal circumstances, this star number brings the kind of triumphs that lead to other opportunities opening up. Unfortunately for the Rooster, in 2019, it is sitting on the *Star of Natural Disaster* brought by the 24 Mountains. So there can be dangers lurking, and since the Rooster's spirit essence is neither weak nor strong, the impact of the 24 Mountains stars in the West is hard to predict when it comes to its effect on the sign.

The other two sectors of the West have the stars of the *Three Killings*, which afflicts both Rooster as well as the astrological-opposite sign of Rabbit in the East. It is important that the *Three Killings* be overcome by placing the **Three Celestial Protectors Windchime** in the West. This ensures the power of the number 1 is not dissipated by the disturbing winds brought by the 24 Mountains.

Three Celestial
Protectors Windchime

OVERCOMING THE THREE KILLINGS

The West is afflicted by the *Three Killings* in 2019, which brings three kinds of problems associated with loss of good fortune. This phenomenon affects only primary directions and this year it has flown to the West. Those who face this direction of 3 Killings will suffer loss of one's good name, loss of loved ones and loss of wealth - very similar to the sufferings heaped on Harvey Weinstein!

In 2019, it occupies the West, so the danger here is to the *youngest daughter* of the family. Anyone occupying the West also suffers this affliction. Place the right kind of cures to effectively dissolve the energy chi of the Three Killings. Doing this is sure to help you avoid whatever nasty consequences that may arise.

In terms of cures, we have been using the ***Three Celestial Protectors*** comprising the ***Chi Lin***, ***Fu Dog*** and ***Pi Yao*** with great success for several years now.

Display the Three Celestial Protectors in the WEST to protect against the energies of the Three Killings affliction.

In 2019, you can continue to use these celestials, this time designed as bejewelled celestial protectors. Placed together, these celestials create a powerful, invisible shield of protective energy that prevents the *Three Killings* from passing into the home or office. In 2019, it is a good idea to keep all West sector doors and windows closed during the afternoon hours, as this blocks the *Three Killings* energy.

IN THE NORTHWEST
#9 MAGNIFYING STAR
(bringing positive frequencies)

In 2019, the number 9 is in the Northwest. This number creates very positive frequencies for everyone sleeping, working or having their main entrance located in the Northwest. The power of 9 is the number that stands for *future prosperity,* so it is the number of the immediate future. The Period of 9 will come in 2024, which is getting near. We should start sowing seeds for future prosperity by activating this FIRE number, which can be regarded as the number indicating wealth luck for the year and for the future.

It is a good idea to start symbolically amassing asset wealth for your family, mainly to benefit the children of the family by creating an asset wealth **Treasure Trove.** Place in the NW this year, or in the SOUTH of the home, either in the living room or under the altar (if you have one in your home) then fill it each year with new gold ingots, coins tied with red thread and lucky wish-granting jewels.

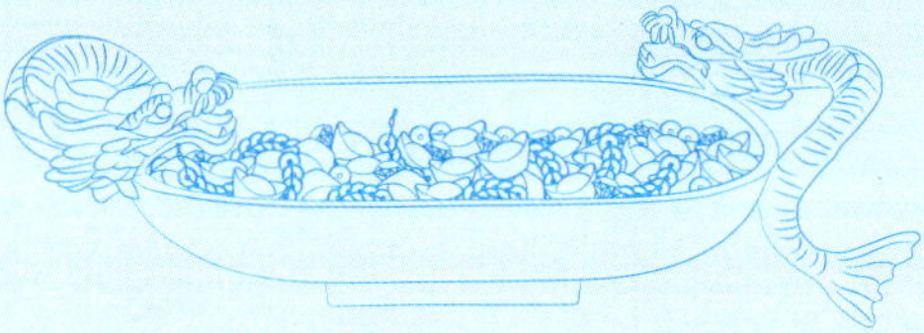

The number 9 will benefit all *Patriarchs* in 2019 and you can energize the power of 9 by making this part of rooms brighter and lighter. Install a **new chandelier** or place **light activators** here to ensure a flow of creative luck for the leader of the family, or the boss of the office.

Note also that there is a *Star of Small Auspicious* in the NW & this can be maximized by placing something supremely auspicious here.

The placement of a spiritually-enhanced symbol to bring out the special significance of the Flying Star number 9 bringing Completion Luck as well as the *Star of Small Auspicious* can be simultaneously energized this year by placing the **Four Great Kings** in this sector of the home, as much to activate the power of this important numeral, as to bring extra luck to the Patriarch.

The Four Great Kings rule the four cardinal directions of the Universe, and they are respected throughout Asia. These are celestial deities that feature in many of the Sutras expounded by the Buddha, who praise the four kings' compassion and enormous power in bringing a variety of benefits to mankind. Inviting and placing the Four Great Kings in the home is one of the best ways for you to add to the auspicious energies of the year.

APPEASING THE TAI SUI

In 2019, the God of the Year, the Tai Sui, moves into the location of the BOAR, which is NW3. Those having their bedroom in this part of the home must NOT sit facing the Tai Sui (i.e. NW3). You should always sit with the Tai Sui behind, supporting you.

In 2019, Tai Sui is helpful to all those born in the year of the BOAR. But he is in direct confrontation with those born in the year of the SNAKE, who could get hurt by this confrontation.

Everyone must be careful never to sit or stand directly facing NW3, especially those born in the

Display the Tai Sui plaque and carry the Tai Sui amulet to get the God of the Year onto your side.

years of the Snake sign. The Snake is visited by the *Star of Sui Po*, which strengthens the negative effects of confronting the Tai Sui. This makes it crucial for those born in years of the Snake to be especially mindful to place a well-carved **Pi Yao** made of some kind of precious stone or a bejewelled Pi Yao in the NW3 location of the home as a peace offering to the Tai Sui.

Advice regarding the Tai Sui is something everyone should take seriously. It is stressed in the famous *Treatise on Harmonizing Times and*

Distinguishing Directions compiled under the patronage of the Qianlong Emperor during the mid-Eighteenth century that the Tai Sui has been recognized for over 2000 years.

According to the Treatise, locations in which the Tai Sui reside or has just vacated are *lucky* locations. In 2019, the whole NW sector is thus considered auspicious, benefitting leaders and father figures of households.

The Treatise explains however that it is *unlucky* when one directly confronts the Tai Sui's residence. It is therefore *unlucky* to "confront" the Tai Sui, i.e. to refrain from facing Northwest 3 through the year.

Thus NW is an inauspicious direction to face, even if it is personally lucky for those for whom the NW is their *sheng chi* direction.

DO NOT CONFRONT TAI SUI!

Confronting the Grand Duke always brings problems and difficulties. When you face the Tai Sui, nothing you do can proceed smoothly. Obstacles surface unexpectedly and even friends turn into adversaries. Thus the Boar must not face its own home direction in 2019 and instead should have its back protected by its direction. This brings the support of the Tai Sui. This means that for the Boar sign, facing Southeast 3 is very lucky. This advice also applies to all others.

To stay on the good side of the Tai Sui, place the **Tai Sui Plaque** in the NW3 location.

It is likewise beneficial to place the beautiful **Pi Yao** in the Northwest 3 sector, as this celestial chimera will bring enormous good fortune, especially when bejewelled and decorative. It is also the best way to gain the support of the God of the Year.

You can also carry the **Tai Sui Amulet of 2019** to be blessed by the Tai Sui this year. Gaining his support benefits your career and brings promotion luck your way.

DOUBLE BOAR "chi lung yap suai"
Place this incredible auspicious wealth symbol to attract serious wealth luck into the home. This activates the power of the Boar for bringing wealth luck into the home. Place the two Boars sitting on the NW2 sector, where the 24 Mountains ***Star of Small Auspicious*** will ensure good fortune comes on a regular basis.

IN THE NORTH
#4 PEACH BLOSSOM STAR
(backed by auspicious 24 Mountains Stars!)

The number that flies into the North brings *Peach Blossom Luck*, which implies that romance is the main force at work here in the North. The star of the Peach Blossom benefits lovers and those who want to find love. The North in 2019 is especially powerful in its impact on the trinity of allies made up of RABBIT, BOAR and SHEEP. These are the three signs for whom the RAT in the North is the Peach Blossom sign. It is thus

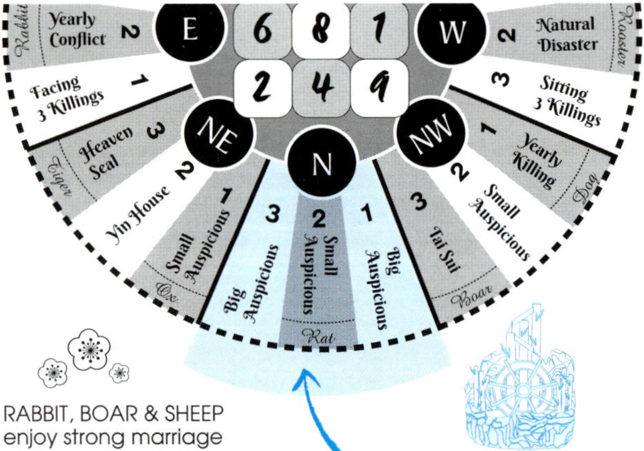

RABBIT, BOAR & SHEEP enjoy strong marriage and romance luck in 2019, and can activate this kind of luck with Peach Blossom RAT.

Place a water feature in the North to capture the auspicious energy here.

not surprising that in 2019, this trinity of signs also benefit from **marriage luck.** Likewise, those whose bedrooms are in the North sector of the home can also enjoy great love and relationship luck. But more than romance luck, the NORTH, enjoys three powerfully auspicious stars brought by the 24 Mountains. Thus there are two stars of *Big Auspicious* flanking one star of *Small Auspicious*. This brings extremely fortunate luck to anyone whose main door is located in the North, or whose bedroom is positioned in this part of the home.

Those whose rooms lie in the NORTH sector of the house will also enjoy tremendous good fortune. Bedrooms in the North will feel this good fortune strongly through the year.

It is extremely beneficial to activate the North sector with a **beautiful water feature.** Cascading water benefits the whole house when such a water feature is placed here. You can use a bubbling water feature or a tabletop waterfall in the North to simulate *yang water energy chi.* Aquariums with healthy fish will also work nicely.

This will activate the three auspicious stars of 24 Mountains. Better yet if you have a lake or a river flowing by this part of your home OR if there is a **swimming pool** or fish pond placed in this part of the home. Anyone born in the year of the Rat will also benefit hugely from the placement of Water here, as it activates the three auspicious stars of the 24 Mountains.

The North sector is extremely auspicious in 2019, and gets activated by yang Water energy. If your bedroom is in the North part of the home, to have a lake, river, swimming pool or any kind of water feature outside your window would be extremely auspicious.

THE AFFLICTED SECTORS of 2019

Make a note of these sectors in your living room, dining room, home office and bedroom. Also pay special attention to the part of your home where the main entrance is located.

1. The **Illness Star 2** is in the NE
2. The **Quarrelsome Star 3** is in the SOUTH
3. The deadly **Five Yellow** is in the SW
4. The **Violent Star 7** is in the SE

Everyone benefits from safeguarding their homes and work places from the feng shui chart afflictions of the year, simply because these afflictions can sometimes be quite deadly. They cause good fortune to get reversed, and when the deadly #5 star is in the SW sector, it is not only very strong, but it also harms the family matriarch, and this can have long term consequences in some households.

The key lies in placing remedies for the bad luck stars and afflictions. What you need to know is where the afflicted winds are, how strong the affliction winds of 2019 are, then place the remedies and cures to suppress these bad winds.

The Art of Placement is the way you can practice Symbolic Feng Shui – which is the easiest method of making sure the energies of your home blend with those of the year. Your personal energies according to your animal sign can also be in sync with those of the year.

When you familiarize yourself with the advice here, you will be forewarned about how to safeguard yourself and your family from the bad energies of the year. When you know what to do, the cures and enhancers will ensure there are powerful good feng shui energies in your home.

You can also refer to our annual FENG SHUI ALMANAC, where we have compiled more detailed information on the good and bad days (and hours) to perform key tasks such as opening a new business, starting renovations, moving house, getting married and signing important contracts. The analysis of the feng shui chart involves assessing the strength of numbers in the different sectors of the living space. The star numbers as well as the 24 Mountains influence each of the animal signs in different ways. Understanding the stars and numbers and their combinations with the elements of sectors and animal signs gives us the luck profile of each of the signs, and each of the sectors of any space.

This merging of Chinese astrology with feng shui is summarized into these books, which we research, compile and write every year. There is nothing else like these books out there in the market place, but there are "copies" of bits and pieces of these books. Be careful, because the charts need to be analyzed and interpreted correctly, and remedies and enhancers need to be made accurately.

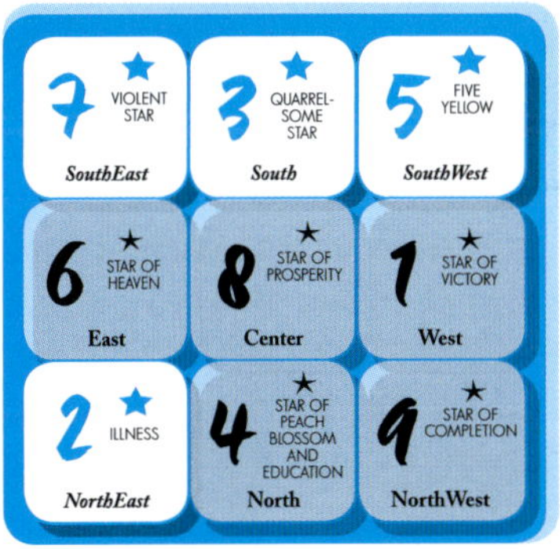

Beware the sectors with afflicted stars in 2019. Important to place subduing cures before the start of the year.

Afflicted sectors in 2019

IN THE NORTHEAST
SUBDUING #2 ILLNESS STAR
(strong in 2019)

In 2019, the illness star 2 flies to the NORTHEAST. It resides in the place of the current period and it is an Earth sector – so Earth flies into Earth – which strengthens the effect of the illness star. This means that the illness star here brings serious illness luck to those whose bedrooms are located here, and those whose main doors are located in the Northeast. It also affects those born under the signs of OX and TIGER.

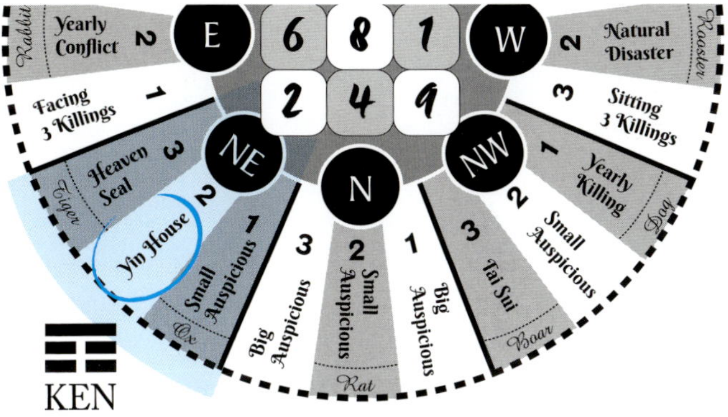

The Northeast is the place of the trigram KEN, which stands for the "mountain", indicating the essence of EARTH Element; and since the ***Illness Star #2*** is also Earth here, this creates a dangerous threat. Be very careful staying in the NE part of any room, and definitely be wary of having your bedroom located in this sector within the house.

The correct remedy needed to suppress the illness star is the **Brass Wu Lou**, which in 2019 must be placed in the NE sector. This is always an effective remedy.

The Wu Lou is one of the most effective cures against illness afflictions. They are best when made of metal.

We also recommend the placement of the **powerful Garuda Windchime** to suppress the nagas that bring illness. Placed in the Northeast, this will totally suppress the star of 2. It will also suppress the star of the *Yin Gate*.

The good news for the NORTHEAST is that in NE1 & NE3, we have two VERY lucky stars, the Small Auspicious & the Heaven Seal respectively.

Garuda Windchime

The Northeast is the astrological location of the signs of the Ox and Tiger, and in 2019, both signs have lucky stars brought to them by the 24 Mountains. To capture the good fortune stars in the NE, we recommend placing the **Golden Deities Heaven Seal** here.

Place the Golden Deities Heaven Seal in the NE3 to benefit from heaven's blessings and benefactor luck in 2019.

Place this in NE3 to attract heaven's blessings, which always comes in the form of *qui ren* luck! Notice we have drawn the **Immortal Sage sitting on the Tiger.** *Qui ren* luck is one of the most auspicious of good fortune energies.

It is also beneficial to activate with an Auspicious Star Energizer to be placed in the location of the Ox i.e. in NE1. Here we suggest the image of the **Sacred Cow** with 8 Auspicious Objects and 7 Royal Emblems. This enhancer brings enormous wealth luck, and it will come in a sure but steady flow.

The Sacred Cow is decorated with the 8 Auspicious Objects, and the 7 Royal Emblems.

Things to do in 2019 if you live in a HOUSE facing or sitting NORTHEAST, or in a NE-located room:

- Keep lights at the front door dim to avoid strengthening the #2 star
- Place **Garuda Wu Lou** and **Windchimes** in the foyer area to suppress the illness star
- Place bejewelled **Blue Medicine Buddha** and **Garuda** in NE2
- Paint the door or wall in the NE white to keep the #2 star suppressed
- Place the **Immortal Sage sitting on a Tiger** in NE3 location
- Place **Sacred Cow** in the NE1 location.
- Place the **Longevity God Sau** in the NE sector

The Garuda Wu Lou to suppress the Illness Star.

IN THE SOUTH
SUBDUING #3 QUARRELSOME STAR
(not strong in 2019)

The noisy, quarrelsome star 3 flies to the SOUTH bringing misunderstandings and hostility vibrations here.

This is a deadly star which can turn even the best relationships into abusive and argumentative ones. The #3 star causes fights to break out, problems to get blown out of proportion, and it can even lead to court cases and all sorts of legal entanglements. This star afflicts those who live in bedrooms located in the South and causes problems for those whose home entrances face South.

The number 3 star is a WOOD element star, capable of turning small problems into BIG ones, causing aggravations that can quickly turn serious. Unfortunately, for anyone having a bedroom in the South sector of the house, this year the hostile star 3 will bring them problems indeed.

Fortunately however, this year the #3 star is weak and flying into the South makes it weaker. Here, we see the WOOD element flying into a FIRE sector, and since Fire consumes Wood, the #3 star gets consumed by the Fire energy. As a result of this configuration of elements, the animal sign afflicted i.e. the HORSE, which is intrinsically FIRE energy, can also subdue the #3 star on its own.

The SOUTH is the astrological home of the HORSE, and here the #3 star is weak in the face of the sign's FIRE energy.

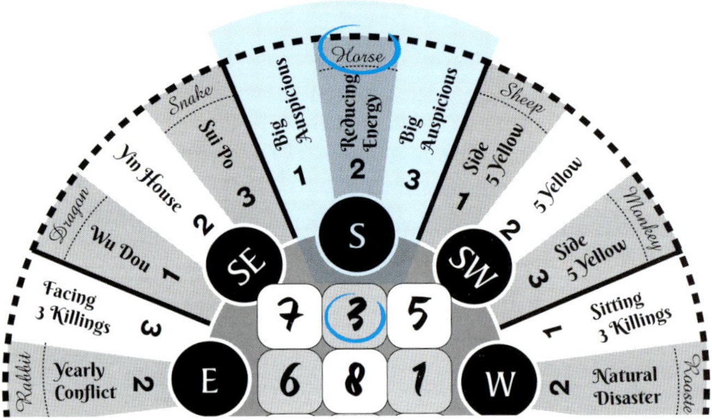

Nevertheless, it is a good idea to keep the #3 star subdued, and this can be done by burning incense inside a **red coloured incense holder,** which you can use to make regular incense offerings to the local spirits who reside in this sector of your home. This will ensure there is no more anger energy in the home, as the incense offering will appease all the local spirits, hence keeping all quarrelsome or litigious energies out of the way. Even small misunderstandings will be a thing of the past.

Things to do in 2019 if you live in a SOUTH-facing house

- Do NOT place water near the front door, as this strengthens the number 3 star
- Turn on lights at the front of the house and keep the foyer area well-lit.
- Burn incense daily in a **red coloured incense container** near main door.
- Place water at the back of the house to activate the North.
- Place **Four Seasons Tree of Life Red Carpet** in the South.

4 Seasons Tree of Life Red Carpet

IN THE SOUTHWEST
SUBDUING #5 WU WANG STAR
(strong this year)

The Five Yellow or *wu wang* flies to the SOUTHWEST in 2019, bringing misfortune luck that can and often does cause reversals of fortunes to families.

This star afflicts those whose main door or bedroom is located in the SW. Anyone occupying a room here will also feel the misfortune luck of the Five Yellow. This is a feng shui situation that is viewed with nervousness by anyone well-versed in feng shui, and because it is an Earth element number, it easily dominates the Southwest, which is also an Earth element sector. The Five Element cure used to combat the Five Yellow needs to be very powerful this year.

Those born in years of the SHEEP and MONKEY especially must suppress this deadly Five Yellow star. These are the astrological signs directly hit by this very fierce affliction in 2019. Carry the **Tri-coloured Five Element Pagoda** all through the year to protect yourself against its pernicious energies and also make sure you have placed this pagoda in the Southwest of your living room.

It is absolutely necessary to suppress the unpleasant effects of this toxic number in the SW to prevent it from spreading to other parts of the house. This star is very strong in 2019, hence this year's Five Element Pagoda remedy needs to likewise be very strong.

The most powerful remedy for this year's *wu wang* is the Tri-coloured Five Element Pagoda. This year's pagoda will efficiently subdue the *wu wang* star also known as the Five Yellow this year. The three colours of Metal is needed, as the *wu wang* is an Earth star and in an Earth sector is very strong. The Pagoda is further strengthened with the wish-granting mantra at its base. When you place this pagoda in the SW sector of your room, think strongly that the OM AH HUM and mantra on its base seamlessly transforms the *Five Yellow* affliction in the SW sector into blessings.

Place this remedy in the SW of the living room. If you have several levels in your home, it is beneficial to place one ***miniature pagoda*** at each level or in each room. These miniature pagodas need the main pagoda on the ground level to ensure it can help spread the energy from the main pagoda. The best is to get a main pagoda for the ground level, and then to get extra mini pagodas for other levels of the home.

Another powerful cure that can dispel all dark forces from the Five Yellow in 2019 when the Earth energy gets so afflicted is the powerful remedy known as the **Vajra Armour Protection Mirror**. If you have an altar in your home, place this remedy on the altar. Otherwise, place high on a side cabinet. This is a powerful cure that can totally subdue all evil intentions and bad feelings, keeping bad energy from entering the home.

The Vajra Armour Protection Mirror dissolves all misfortune luck. If you or your family are going through really tough times associated with a reversal of fortune, a broken relationship, a loss of income stream (such as losing your job) or a serious illness which just cannot get cured, this is a powerful remedy.

Do note that the Five Yellow brings severe illness, accidents and loss that manifest in a variety of ways. It is the catalyst for all kinds of misfortune, and when you feel its afflictions, it is as if your life suddenly collapses all around you. When you read about tragedies striking a family, you can be sure that the Five Yellow is in some way responsible, either because it afflicts the main door, or the room occupied by the victim.

If your main door, bedroom or office desk is afflicted by the Five Yellow due to their location in the SW, this affliction must be dealt with before 4th February 2019. Do not be careless or forget about it, as bad luck caused by the Five Yellow can take effect very quickly. Prevention is better than cure, so do not wait until it is too late. You must also check where the Five Yellow flies to each month.

For those born in TIGER years, you must be extra careful in the months of FEBRUARY and NOVEMBER, as these are the months when the Five Yellow flies into your month chart. You also have the annual #2 illness star affliction, which gets exacerbated by the Five Yellow.

Make sure you are protected these months, and that remedies are in place.

Things to do in 2019 if you live in a SOUTHWEST-facing house

- Place the **Tri-coloured Five Element Pagoda** at the front of the house
- Place **Vajra Armour Protection Mirror** inside the house in the foyer area.
- Keep the front lights of the house turned off or dimmed through the year.
- Place **miniature Tri-coloured Five Element Pagodas** on upper floors of home.

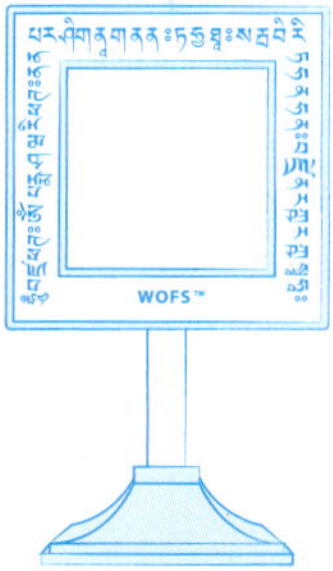

Vajra Armour Protection
Mirror

DO NOT RENOVATE THE SOUTHWEST IN 2019!

It is imperative that everyone observes the NO RENOVATION rule for the SW this year. Any kind of demolition or digging work here is dangerous in 2019, as this causes negative luck to manifest. It is especially dangerous to drill floors, knock down walls, dig holes in the ground, engage in any kind of destructive work or make too much noise.

These activities activate the Five Yellow, which triggers severe misfortune luck to come the way of the household. Protect against this happening. Keep the SOUTHWEST quiet.

If you must undertake renovations in your house and it encroaches into the SW sector, make sure your cures are prominently in place AND make very sure the renovation does not start or end in the SW. No one should be staying in the SW sector when renovations are going on.

IN THE SOUTHEAST
SUBDUING #7 BETRAYAL STAR
(strong this year)

This is an ugly star that brings betrayal, robbery and violence. In 2019, it is located in the SOUTHEAST, which is the place of the eldest daughter and the home location of those born in years of the SNAKE & DRAGON. This is a nasty affliction that affects everyone whose bedroom or main door are located in the Southeast sector of their homes.

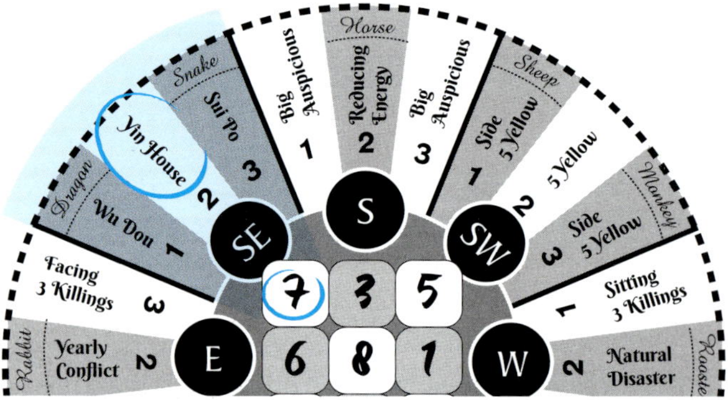

The #7 star brings the threat of violence and burglary, betrayal and loss. This year, in the SE, it is exarcerbated by the *Star of the Yin House* brought by the 24 Mountains. Try to avoid having your important rooms here and also avoid working in this sector this year. If your bedroom or front door is located in the Southeast, it is important to install the cure against this affliction.

Over the years, placing a **Blue Rhinoceros and Elephant** with **Water element motif** and strengthened with a protective mantra proved an excellent repellent against this # 7 star. It worked as prevention against getting robbed and was a good way of ensuring those who used the cure stayed safe from petty burglars.

Another good way to overcome the negative effect of #7 is to have a **large water feature** here, as water exhausts the vitality of 7. Water is also auspicious for the SE and it strengthens the WOOD element here. Those who already have a water feature here, such as a pond in the garden or an internal water feature in the living room, will be happy to know that in addition to generating good fortune luck for the eldest daughter of the family, water here suppresses the #7 star.

In 2019, Water in the SOUTHEAST brings a smoother flow of energies that dispels problems associated with getting robbed or cheated.

We have observed that the #7 star can also cause political turmoil in the work area, creating aggressive behaviour between competing factions in the office. The #7 star brings out the worst in all who come under its influence. And in 2019, having flown to into a WOOD sector, it can become more dangerous. This is because #7 is a red star and it is also a METAL star. Together, the #7 star spells violence; some astrologers refer to it as the *Star of the Soldier* associating it with weapons and bloodshed. It is lethal in the Southeast because Metal destroys Wood!

This year, the best way to suppress the #7 Metal star which can cause your house to get burgled is to use this Wall Amulet which activates the combination of FIRE and WATER together. Here, Water exhausts and Fire destroys the negative aspects of #7's Metal. The two elements are a powerful manifestation of the Water element turning into steam from the heat of Fire. Here, the amulet prevents burglary of any kind.

Anti-Burglary Plaque

Hang this Wall Amulet outside your home or apartment to prevent bad people gaining entry into your home.

Remember that in life, betrayal manifests in many different ways & it is often heartbreaking when it happens. Betrayal luck is brought by the #7 star & it is worthwhile guarding against it happening.

Note also that in the year 2019, the Luck Stars of the 24 Mountains reflect the "stars" placed in the opposite direction of Northwest. The most important thing to take note of is the *Sui Po Star*, which is in SE3, the place of the SNAKE that is in direct conflict with the Tai Sui. It is important that the amulet plaque to appease the Tai Sui be placed in this sector of SE3. This protects the sector as well as the sign of the Snake.

In SE2, we have the 24 Mountains star of *Yin House* which needs to be suppressed with strong yang energy; keeping the Southeast location well-lit during night time is an excellent way of dispelling the *yin* forces brought by this star. Note that in our *yang* dwellings, we should always

Take note of the Sui Po star, which is in SE3, the place of the SNAKE that is in direct conflict with the TAI SUI.

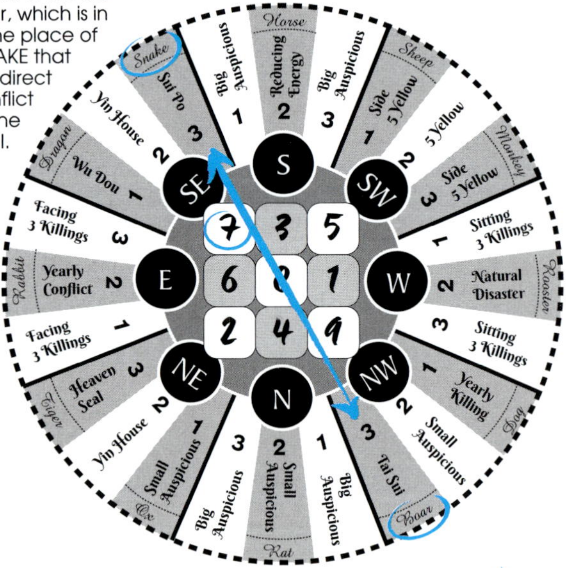

guard against *yin spirit formation*. So it really is beneficial to **light a candle** each day in the Southeast sector.

Things to do in 2019 if you live in an SOUTHEAST facing house

- Place **water in a red container** in this sector
- Place a **water feature** just inside or outside the main door
- Paint your front wall **blue** to simulate water chi energy
- Place **Anti-Burglary Plaque** to protect against break-ins
- Display **Red-faced Kuan Kung** in the SE of the house to protect against all forms of loss and harm

Red-faced Kuan Kung

Chapter Two

GENERAL LUCK FOR THE SIGN OF THE TIGER

Seal of Heaven brings celestial support in 2019

Those born in the year of the Tiger will benefit from excellent levels of energetic life force in 2019 and this is complemented by exceptionally powerful spirit essence. These two categories in your luck profile will enable you to rise above all challenges, imbuing you with a can-do attitude that attracts success and abundance.

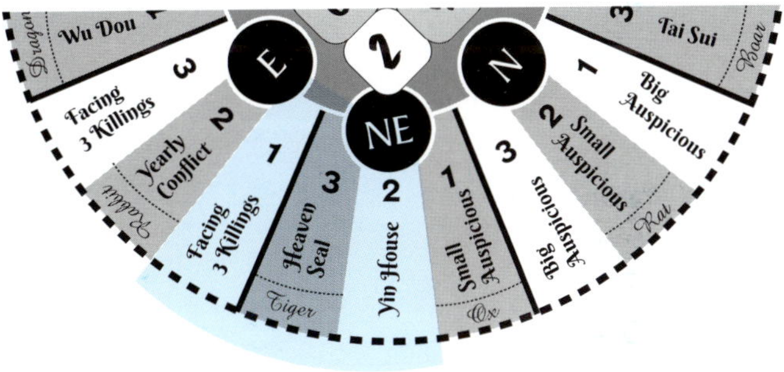

In personal feng shui astrology, nothing brings greater strength than knowing that your outer and inner vitally levels are high. This enables you to stand firm and resolute, a proud warrior who allows few things to dampen your spirit. This is all the more extraordinary as your personal *lung ta* is very weak in 2019. There is little success luck indicated, but with such a strong spirit essence and life force, all you need to increase your level of success luck is to bring in **Windhorse activators** into your living space. Here, the symbolic presence of the Windhorse will empower your **lung ta** – and if you can send Windhorse flags into the skies, this will benefit you even more.

This is also a year when inviting **King Gesar** sitting on the Windhorse into your home is most timely, and sending Windhorse balloons into the skies to seek success luck from the celestials is also very appropriate.

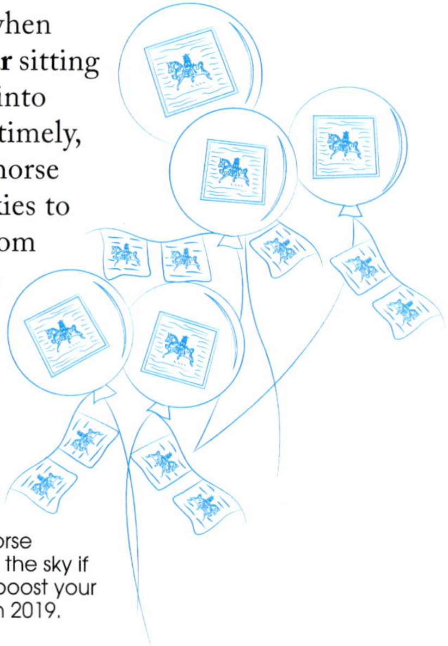

Send Windhorse balloons into the sky if you can, to boost your low lung ta in 2019.

Tiger plays host to HEAVENLY SEAL

This is a year when the Tiger plays host to the *Heavenly Seal*, which brings you powerful celestial support. The Chinese have always believed that when this potent 24 Mountains star comes into your compass location, that is when you have the sacred approval of the God of Heaven.

The God of Heaven

You then benefit from hidden help that is subtle and effective for all your endeavours to succeed. This assistance comes from heaven. It is unseen and invisible. It is the *Seal of Heaven* and it can override whatever negative indications may show up in other charts affecting the Tiger sign.

ELEMENT LUCK OF THE

2019	Year Element	Earth Tiger *81/21 years*	Metal Tiger *69/9 years*
LIFE FORCE	WATER	Excellent OOO	Excellent OOO
HEALTH	WOOD	Very Bad XX	Bad X
WEALTH	EARTH	Good O	Excellent OOO
SUCCESS (*LUNG TA*)	FIRE	Very Bad XX	Very Bad XX
SPIRIT ESSENCE	METAL	Excellent OOO	Excellent OOO

TIGER IN 2019

Water Tiger *57 years*	Wood Tiger *45 years*	Fire Tiger *33 years*
Excellent OOO	Excellent OOO	Excellent OOO
Very Good OO	Neutral OX	Excellent OOO
Very Bad XX	Very Good OO	Neutral OX
Very Bad XX	Very Bad XX	Very Bad XX
Excellent OOO	Excellent OOO	Excellent OOO

From your element luck profile, you can see that your 2019 luck indications are very extreme. There is excellent body capability (life force) and mental strength (spirit essence) but success potential lacks strength. Your *lung ta* is very weak.

And in the case of the **57-year-old Water Tiger,** whose wealth luck profile is extremely weak, you must pay close attention to the outflow of prosperity affecting you. This is a year to be very careful.

You might suffer financial loss or experience economic instability in 2019, so you must be extra careful. Do not take risks in investments, and definitely do not over indulge or overspend this year.

The **81-year-old Earth Tiger** meanwhile is at some risk of coming down with a serious illness. You must rest and do only the gentlest of exercises, because for you, health indications are extremely dangerous. The **21-year-old Earth Tiger** being young and strong is at less of a health risk. Nevertheless, it is prudent to take things easy and be mindful of your health.

Afflicted by the ILLNESS STAR

The Tiger's home location of Northeast is hit by the year's illness star. This brings winds that make everyone born under this sign vulnerable to the naga forces of the Earth. This makes you susceptible to bacterial infections and virus strains that bring painful illnesses of various kinds. It is a good year to be open to taking vitamin supplements that strengthen your immune systems.

The illness star *must* be subdued with the use of feng shui remedies.

Here, the most important symbol to have in your home is the **wu lou**, which you should display in your home sector, which is the Northeast corner of your bedroom or living room. This has always been the traditional cure for overcoming the feng shui illness star. For something stronger, you can display the **Garuda Wu Lou**, as this gives added potency to subduing the illness-bringing nagas; and even better, if you have an altar in your home, invite the **Medicine Buddha** into your home.

The Tiger is known to possess great inner strength, strong intelligence and the kind of determination that gets things done. You are also fiercely protective of loved ones and especially of your children. In 2019, this characteristic will be more evident than ever. Tiger people do seem intimidating at first, but you make a wonderful and loyal friend, although you can be selective as to whom you allow into your inner group of good friends.

For the Tiger, this is not a year to be ambitious. It is better to cultivate patience, refrain from taking too many risks and bide your time. This is also not a good year to make too many changes to the pattern and rhythm of your life.

Stay cool! Stay patient! Stay careful! When things seem rough, do not complain, and when obstacles cause you to lose time or productivity, do not try to explain! You should however stay positive and not let illness obstacles or mishaps in the family distract you too much. There will be difficulties that make you realize you are vulnerable to the luck energies of the year. Be comforted by the fact that hidden forces are helping you; and your physical and mental health are at the highest levels.

Carry **amulets** this year when you travel. Stick **anti-illness stickers** onto your car windows and place remedies inside your home and in your office at work.

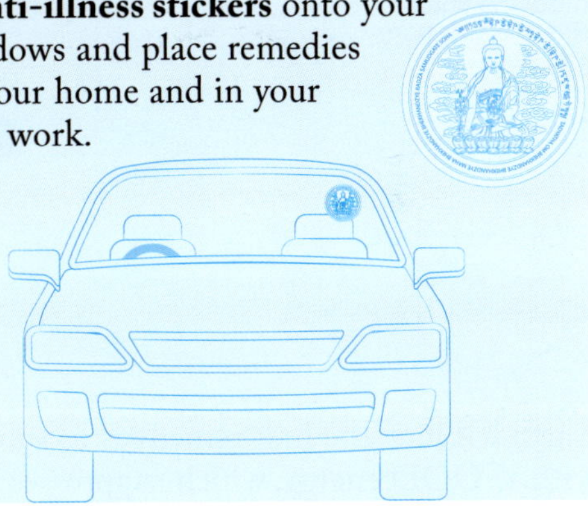

Weathering ILLNESS DISTRACTIONS

While the Tiger must endure a year of illness distractions caused by the illness star brought by the feng shui winds of the year, yours is an animal sign that resides in a secondary sector, so the impact of this star is less strong. To overcome the #2's illness vibrations, you need to reduce the strength of Earth element energy. This is because this is a star whose element is EARTH, and being in the NE, the illness star is in its own

The Tiger sign benefits from having plants and fresh flowers in the home, whose WOOD element energy will combat the illness EARTH energies from the #2 star.

Earth habitat. The best remedy is to subdue it with WOOD energy, which suppresses Earth energy. Thus having **plants** here brings healthy growth luck. Also, make an effort to have a regular display of **fresh flowers** in the NE sector of the home, as these are a good antidote to the #2 star.

Hang **metal windchimes** with the **wu lou symbol** and carry the **Garuda Amulet** to subdue all illness energies so they do not distract you. The Tiger sign is extremely strong this year and this makes you a lot less vulnerable to the illness star affliction.

HEALTH LUCK of the 5 Element Tigers

- For the **9-year-old Metal Tiger** child, carry the **Garuda Amulet** at all times. The Tiger child is especially vulnerable to illness this year.
- The **21-year-old Earth Tiger** must be careful to stay protected against the illness star, as your health luck is very bad this year. Place anti-illness cures near you and wear the **Wu Lou pendant**.
- The **33-year-old Fire Tiger** can display a **Wu Lou with Ruyi symbol** to take fullest advantage of your excellent life force this year.
- The **45-year-old Wood Tiger** must hang lots of **windchimes** and the Patriarchs among you are advised to carry the **Garuda Amulet**.
- The **57-year-old Water Tiger** has very good health luck. You are the least vulnerable to the Illness Star.

Garuda Amulet

OUTLOOK FOR THE
81/21 YEAR OLD EARTH TIGER

The Earth Tiger should avoid rocky terrain this year. This is because this Tiger is particularly vulnerable to the naga spirits residing in rocky mountain areas. Your health luck is at a very low level and your spiritual immunity is also not high.

You need to wear or carry the **Garuda Anti-Illness Amulet** as this adds the spiritual dimension to your strong physical disposition inner essence.

The older Tiger should definitely take things easy this year, while the 21-year-old will benefit from adopting a humble disposition. This brings celestial luck your way. In 2019, you should ensure that night time outings are reduced as you have the *Yin House Star* on your right and you are close to the poisons coming from the *Three Killings Star* on your left.

The Earth Tiger in 2019 enjoys good wealth but very bad health luck. Your personal *lung ta* is very weak, so you have no success luck this year. The most outstanding thing about your luck profile is that your Life Force and Spirit Essence are both at an excellent level. This means you can withstand all kinds of challenges. In 2019, you will feel positive and powerful. Few things can push you off course. The intrinsic Wood element of the Tiger makes you sharp and alert; you will have great creativity that brings added power to your work. The Earth element brings you power and authority, so together, your combination of elements in 2019 suggests your own intellect will lift you high. You are very young and any elevation to your status comes from your own effort. Remember to stay humble at all times.

This is a year when your energy levels are a good level. You feel strong and eager to take on new challenges. Career luck brings you good elevation luck at work, so do not be surprised if you should get some quick promotion this year. Your sign is strong and you have natural resistance to harmful spirits. This is because your spirit essence and life force are both at excellent levels of strength.

The 21-year-old Tiger should wear or carry the **Windhorse Amulet**. This amulet helps elevate your personal lung ta, enabling you to benefit from success luck.

OUTLOOK FOR THE 57 YEAR OLD WATER TIGER

Those born under this sign must be extra careful with money in 2019, as this dimension of your luck is at a very low level. You must take care not to overspend or be excessively indulgent with yourself this year.

There is real danger of loss of wealth due to bad investments or because of bad gambling luck this year. Your sign needs to carry the **Wealth Activation Amulet**.

Do not get cheated by people with bad intentions, especially those who might be jealous of you at work. It is a good thing that your health luck is at a very good level, as this makes you less vulnerable to those who may use office politics to get you into trouble. It is good that both your life force and spirit essence are at excellent levels. These luck indications make you strong through the year. But do carry the **Protection of Wealth and Good Name** talisman.

Your luck profile based on your element combinations with those of the year indicate that your health luck is very good but your wealth luck is very bad. This almost always suggests loss, so be careful when investing or gambling. The Water Tiger can benefit from good networking luck, but you need to use patience and clever strategizing to win over friends and colleagues.

This is an excellent year to invite assistance from the **Four Great Kings** by displaying their presence in your home. These four kings will help you manifest good fortune, ensuring you take fullest advantage of the year's excellent luck profile shown in your Element Luck chart.

The Four Great Kings are Guardians of the four directions of North, South East and West and one of them, i.e. the Lord of the North, is the Lord of the Yakshas (Wealth Gods of the world) and he guards the Treasures of the Universe.

The other kings carry a ukulele, pagoda, sword and snake, so they protect against various air, wind, earth, water and fire disasters. They also protect against different kinds of loss and against localized spirits with ill intentions who bring bad luck, suffering and illness.

Invite the Four Great Kings into your home to manifest good fortune and to take fullest advantage of the Tiger's excellent luck profile this year.

OUTLOOK FOR THE
45 YEAR OLD WOOD TIGER

The Wood Tiger enjoys very good wealth luck in this year of the Earth Boar, with winnings coming from a windfall, or a rise in the value of your investments. The Wood Tiger is a materialistic sign and has a powerful desire to make big money, more so than any of the other Tiger signs, but you are also extra creative and clever this year.

There are good prospects to grow your wealth this year, but you need to be careful when it comes to making money via new business projects or expansion. Your *lung ta* or success luck is low. The best way to add wealth is via clever investments! Activate the *Heaven Seal* by wearing the **Wealth Amulet** and displaying symbolic **Treasure Chests** next to a **framed picture of yourself** on a table in the NE.

These symbolic enhancers will bring you plenty of speculative wealth luck. You can also display the **Maneki Neki Cat Treasure Chest**. These are made in the Fire element colour of red, which will contribute to activating for wealth luck to come your way.

The two lucky stars in the Tiger's sector will benefit this 45-year-old Tiger in terms of adding to your wealth luck. This year, your luck profile according to your element combinations with that of the year indicate that your wealth luck is very good! As such, you can be an active investor in the stock market.

Using symbolic enhancers to activate your wealth luck will ensure that your overall income increases.

Unfortunately for the Wood Tiger, your success luck is at a very low level, so this year, don't get distracted hoping to count on attaining great heights of success or achievement. Stay cool enjoying life. And rejoice that your life force and spirit essence are at excellent levels - this means you have extremely strong vitality in 2019. Time out then to enjoy life. You are also not vulnerable to bad spirits.

FIRE IN 2019 BRINGS WEALTH

This year, the element that stands for wealth luck is Fire. Lighting red candles decorated with the 8 auspicious signs is an excellent way to add to your wealth luck. You are sitting on the *Star of Heavenly Seal*, thus sending light offerings from red candles is an incredibly effective way to direct wealth luck towards you.

Making light offerings daily using this specially designed candle benefits everyone in 2019 – this magnifies Fire energies, bringing wealth and financial benefits. We have made this candle to last 24 hours to ensure prosperity luck is with you through all hours of the day.

Light offerings from red candles are an effective way to direct wealth energies towards you in 2019.

OUTLOOK FOR THE
33 YEAR OLD FIRE TIGER

The 33-year-old Tiger can be fiery and volatile, usually prone to a hot and quick temper, but in 2019, the influence of the *Heavenly Seal Star* has a calming impact on your disposition. Nevertheless, this Tiger can be impatient, manifesting difficult behaviour that can cause mental distress. However, your health luck is excellent, and this refers to both physical and mental health. Better to direct your vigour and vitality towards your work.

Whatever you may be involved in doing, this is a year when your **energy levels** are at excellent levels. This gives you the strength and determination to set the groundwork on which to build something substantial. It all depends on you.

In terms of prosperity luck, this is a year when everything boils down to your own aspirations. If you have the determination to work towards setting the foundation for big wealth to come to you, this is possible. This is a good year to aim high, to think big and to use your youth and creativity to map out a strategy for success. To ensure that accomplishment luck can ripen over the course of the next few years, you should map out strategies conducive to your level of expertise and capabilities.

To bring you future success in a big way, this is an excellent year to invite into your home this beautiful **Dzambhala Mandala**. This creates for your home the seeds for wealth to take root, germinate and grow, because the five Dzambhalas will imbue your environment with prosperity-activating vibrations.

The Fire Tiger should rejoice that its Life Force and Spirit Essence are at excellent levels, which are so conducive to inviting this **Celestial Mandala of the Wealth Buddhas** into your home. This brings into your surroundings very auspicious forces that will make it easy for you to attain heights of great success when the right time ripens. You can continue to make strides building your future either as a rising executive within a big corporation or in building your own business. Your strong vitality puts you in a good position to enjoy your life, as you do not have to cope with too many difficulties or mishaps.

Here's the thing about the Fire Tiger's outlook luck in the year of the Earth Boar.

The Fire element in your heavenly stem brings you BIG WEALTH LUCK this year, because Fire energy represents prosperity luck.

Meanwhile, in your luck profile for the year, it indicates that the luck to gain wealth depends entirely on your own efforts and aspirations. This is because your combination of elements for wealth luck is showing neutral! This added to your very low *lung ta* indicates you cannot depend on luck alone to get rich. You need to empower your own mind in order to attain lasting success. Use this year to start climbing the career ladder in seriousness; train yourself to work hard and achieve results despite obstacles and lack of luck. Depend on your excellent spirit essence to push yourself forward and upward!

To help you attract wealth luck, burn the **Red Candle with 8 Auspicious Objects** as often as you want to generate yang energy wealth luck. To attract success, strengthen your personal *lung ta* by displaying or wearing the **Windhorse**.

Using the art of placement to make up for the lack of personal wealth and success luck can work wonders in activating positive energies around you.

But most of all, in 2019, you should display the **Auspicious Double Boar** because here, you are generating the power of your secret friend association with the Boar to bring you additional luck of abundance!

Another symbolic placement is to bring into the home is the **4 Seasons Tree of Life Red Carpet.** Placed at the front of the home to welcome in prosperity, this is excellent feng shui for your interiors.

OUTLOOK FOR THE
69 YEAR OLD METAL TIGER

The Metal Tiger has a short temper and can be ferocious when riled. In its old age, the stubborn side of this Tiger is likely to show itself quite often this year. This is a difficult Tiger indeed, as the Metal element in its heavenly stem will most likely cause it to stiffen up and be tougher than ever to deal with.

This is because health luck is not good this year, and it is made worse by the feng shui winds which also brings the Illness Star; hence there will aches, pains and some level of discomfort this year. Although there are not that many other problems, this Tiger can turn out unpleasant to deal with.

In 2019, the Metal element brings power and authority, so others will bend backwards to accommodate your eccentricities.

Note that both your spirit essence and life force are at excellent levels, and this means that your inner and outer strength are very strong. You will always have your way, and this may not always be a good thing. Note that the Metal element in your heavenly stem can bring out your arrogant side. It makes your aura bright and your determination to have your way very strong indeed.

Your stem element makes you fearless, so you push ahead to have others do your bidding. Those amongst you who are healthy and strong will want to pursue your own goals. For you, adding to your prosperity is foremost in your mind.

The indication for wealth luck in your element luck profile is at an excellent level; it matches your life force and spirit essence, so it is likely you can be as alert and as full of vitality as you wish, and if accumulating wealth is your passion, absolutely go for it!

Just remember that your luck profile indicates that your *lung ta* is very bad; you have little "success luck" this year. Although this should not hurt too much at your age, as at 69 years old, it is not success luck that you need. What you need is the vigour and vitality that gives your life force and spirit essence the power to overcome the illness winds of your home location as well as your low level of health luck in your luck profile.

For sure, you must place anti-illness antidotes around your living space. But your obsession with accumulating wealth continues, so it is a good idea to strengthen your wealth accumulation luck. You can do this by displaying the **Four Seasons Tree of Life Red Carpet**. Display near the front of your home or in the Northeast sector of your living area.

The Metal Tiger can be dogmatic, and you tend to be stubborn this year. Carrying the **Anti-Illness Amulet** and living with this red carpet near you will not only bring you wealth luck, it will also subdue your rigid behaviour. Indeed, this is the best way to bring out the best in you.

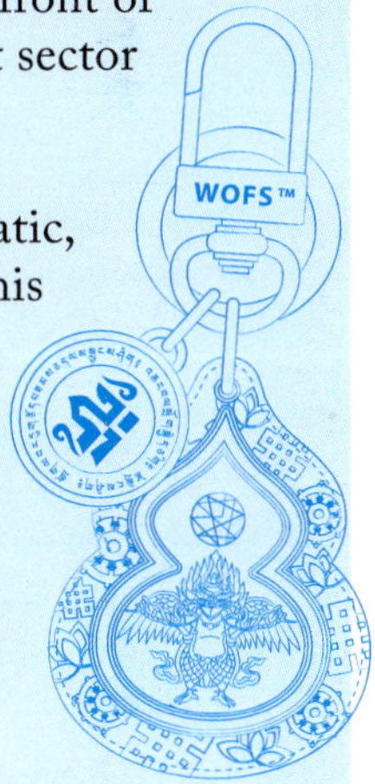

The Fire energy will reduce the inflexibility of your attitude towards those wanting to help you, and contribute significantly to your success.

Chapter Three

TIGER INTERACTING WITH OTHER SIGNS IN 2019

TIGER COMPATIBILITY WITH OTHER SIGNS IN 2019

PAIRINGS	COMPATIBILITY in 2019
TIGER & RAT	Danger of outside interference
TIGER & OX	Good year to discover each other
TIGER & TIGER	Equally enthusiastic
TIGER & RABBIT	Connected by Heavenly Chi
TIGER & DRAGON	Ho Tu combination
TIGER & SNAKE	Mismatched energies
TIGER & HORSE	Patience gets tested
TIGER & SHEEP	No resilience
TIGER & MONKEY	Growling into thin air
TIGER & ROOSTER	Formidable pair
TIGER & DOG	Friendship & Love
TIGER & BOAR	Secret Friends

CHAPTER THREE

THE TIGER INTERACTING WITH OTHER SIGNS IN 2019

Those wanting love will need to work on it

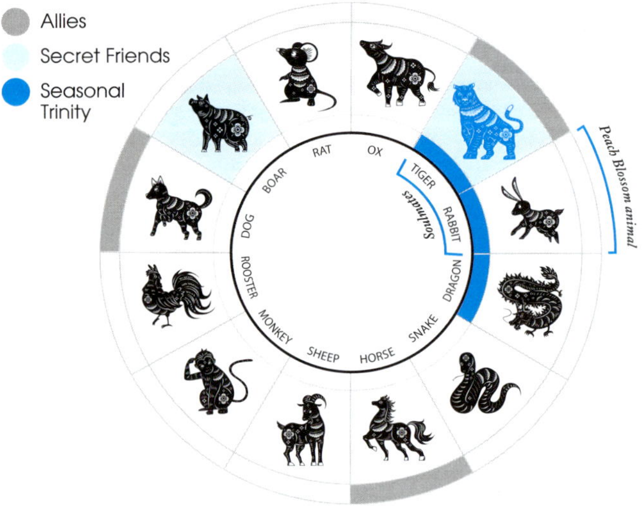

In Chinese Astrology, a variety of influences can and do affect the way you interact and get on with the people around you, your partner, your parents, children, siblings, relatives and friends. Understanding astrological compatibilities can improve all the relationships that are important to you, making life less aggravating and more harmonious.

You understand people's sensitivities better; and you find that it is natural to have greater affinity with some than with others. You might even feel aversion to some people, finding fault with them for the smallest provocation.

The quality of your relationships boil down to astrological affinities that manifest as the trinity of allies, the pairs of secret friends, the twosomes that are zodiac soul mates and more! There are other affinity groupings but these three exert the strongest influences on how you respond to other signs and explain the special feelings you have for some people.

COMPATIBILITY GROUPINGS

1. ALLIANCE OF ALLIES - brings great support
2. POWERFUL SOULMATES - power friendship
3. SECRET FRIENDS - influencing each other
4. ZODIAC ENEMIES - astrological foes
5. PEACH BLOSSOM LINKS - romance
6. SEASONAL TRINITY - wealth-enhancing

1. ALLIANCE OF ALLIES

The Tiger is in the Alliance of Righteous signs with the Dog and the Horse. They are part of the four alliances of allies in the Chinese Zodiac; each alliance comprising three animal signs who share similar moral outlooks, adopt righteous causes and exhibit particular characteristic traits that bond them strongly. These signs tend to be proud of being morally upright; they support each other's aims and often activists adopting and supporting causes they deem are ethical. Of the three, the Tiger is the least political; you are drawn to highly principled people.

COMPETITORS	RAT	DRAGON	MONKEY	Ambitious, Brilliant, Tough
INTELLECTUALS	OX	SNAKE	ROOSTER	Generous, Focused, Resilient
RIGHTEOUS	**DOG**	**TIGER**	**HORSE**	**Ethical, Brave, Loyal**
DIPLOMATS	BOAR	SHEEP	RABBIT	Creative, Kind, Emotional

When all three signs enjoy good fortune in any year, the energy of the alliance is powerful and if all three are present amongst members of a family such as amongst siblings, or between spouse and child, the family presents a very united front. They support one another, and when they prosper, good fortune gets multiplied. Families that have this Alliance of allies are a formidable force and they will tend to be active in do good causes.

Allies always get along well and in a love relationship they make for compatible couples. They trust one another and immediately close ranks in the face of external threats.

Good personal feng shui comes from displaying the symbolic image of your astrological allies. In 2019, the alliance of Tiger, Dog and Horse all benefit from carrying or displaying **images of each other** beside the **mighty red Windhorse** as all three signs of this alliance have very low levels of *lung ta* energy.

These three signs need the help of the Windhorse which can be made strong by displaying the image of this red horse flying into the cosmic heavens bringing success luck. The Windhorse will also be instrumental in smoothing out all the relationships that are important to you through the year, ensuring success comes to you easily. Having an enhanced *lung ta* brings you the Tiger and its allies very precious success luck.

As a team then, your success luck will be increased. The Tiger meanwhile is also sitting on the *Star of Heavenly Seal*, and this brings the powerful assistance of the cosmic heavens. It is definitely beneficial to activate this sacred star of the 24 mountains.

MIXED LIFE FORCE

The Tiger and its allies have mixed levels of life force in 2019. This alliance can collectively rely on the Tiger whose Life Force is excellent hence bringing strength to the alliance. Your spirit essence is also excellent this year. Indeed, the Tiger is only one of two signs with such high levels of these two important aspects of your annual luck dimension. This brings great strength to your inner and outer energy levels. You will be up to all challenges this year. You also have the right amount of willpower to see through all the causes and projects you give your word to.

The Horse has very low levels while the Dog is also enjoying just a neutral level. But the Tiger is hit by the illness star in 2019 and this can cause your vitality levels to decrease in strength. Yet yours is the strongest link in this Alliance. The Tiger also has the strongest star of the 24 mountains.

So it does appear you are the lynchpin of this alliance in 2019.

2. ASTROLOGICAL SOULMATES

There are six pairs of animal signs who are soul mates to each other. They find happiness with each other naturally and easily. One sign is yin, while the other yang.

In astrology texts, they are described as creating six Zodiac Houses with each enjoying its own special niche of compatibility. There is powerful bonding at a cosmic level and any marriage or business union between any two soul mates should end in great happiness as they enjoy great rapport.

The strength of every pair is different, as some make better commercial partners than marriage partners. How successful you are as a pair depends on how deeply you bond and how close you allow yourselves to get with each other.

The Tiger and Rabbit together create the House of Growth and Development.

Here the Tiger employs force while the Rabbit uses diplomacy as their respective ways of getting things done. Professionally, or as a couple in a relationship or as siblings, they get things moving forward.

This is a strong alliance which can do well in 2019. Tiger's energy levels combine well with the feng shui chart's *Heavenly Star* flying into Rabbit's home location. The pairing is advantageous to both irrespective of whatever kind of partnership they get into, be it professional or personal. The Tiger can always depend on Rabbit's sweet talking diplomacy to get it out of trouble. And even though Tiger might fall sick, nevertheless the sign of the Rabbit will always respect its special relationship with the Tiger.

ANIMALS	YIN/ YANG	ZODIAC HOUSE CREATED	TALENTS UNLEASHED
RAT	YANG	House of Creativity and Cleverness	The RAT initiates
OX	YIN		The Ox completes
TIGER	YANG	House of Growth and Development	The TIGER employs Force
RABBIT	YIN		The RABBIT uses diplomacy
DRAGON	YANG	House of Magic and Spirituality	The DRAGON creates Magic
SNAKE	YIN		The SNAKE creates Mystery
HORSE	YANG	House of Passion and Sexuality	The HORSE embodies male energy
SHEEP	YIN		The SHEEP is the female energy
MONKEY	YANG	House of Career and Commerce	The MONKEY creates strategy
ROOSTER	YIN		The ROOSTER gets things moving
DOG	YANG	House of Domesticity	The DOG works to provide
BOAR	YIN		The BOAR enjoys what is created

3. SECRET FRIENDS

Secret friends of the Zodiac are exceptionally compatible. They are a vigorous union of two equals and they are at their best as a married couple. There is love, respect and goodwill between them and their bond, once forged, is hard to break. And even when they themselves want to break up, it will be hard for either party to walk away.

This pair of signs will stick together through thick and thin. They are fiercely protective of each other and even when they are not partners, there is comradeship and simpatico between them.

The secret friend of the Tiger is the Boar.

In the pairing of secret friends, the Tiger is paired with the Boar. There is a special bond between these two animal signs and here, it is the Boar that is most helpful to the Tiger. Either sign displaying their secret friend in the home can create excellent energy for growth in prosperity.

4. ASTROLOGICAL ENEMIES

Note that the Tiger's astrological enemy is the Monkey. Your astrological enemy does not necessarily harm you; but the sign can never be of any real help to you. Your elements have what the astrologers refer to as a **Metal/Wood Clash,** which is an element clash. This brings greater harm to the Tiger than to the Monkey.

CURE: It benefits the Tiger who is going out with the Monkey, or married to the Monkey to place the secret friend of the Monkey, which is the **Snake**, in the home. This is sure to bring peace and harmony into the relationship.

The astrological enemy of the Tiger is the Monkey.

There is a six year gap between any two signs of adversaries and any pairing between them cannot benefit either side. They cannot have sincere intentions towards one another.

Marriage between a Monkey and a Tiger cannot lead to lasting happiness, and even if the marriage endures, there is little happiness unless other indications in their respective Paht Chee charts suggest otherwise.

Tigers are advised to refrain from getting involved with a Monkey either as business partners or as lovers as this pairing is likely to lead to problems. In the event of a split, the separation can be acrimonious.

In 2019, the coming together of Tiger and Monkey will lead to misfortune, as the Monkey has the misfortune star of 5 Yellow!

When two opposite signs have a hostile connection and they stay in the same house, they cannot be close. If they are siblings they will not share confidences and they eventually drift apart. If they stay apart, there will not be direct antagonism but they have little in common. In 2019, the coming together of these two signs is very unlucky and inauspicious.

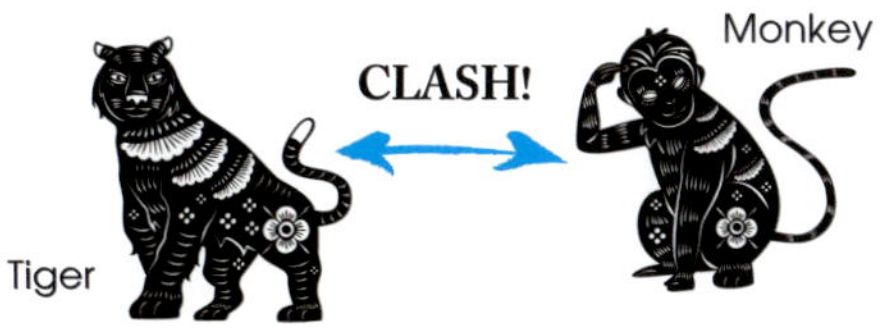

5. PEACH BLOSSOM LINKS

Each of the Alliances of Allies has a special relationship with one of the four primary signs of Horse, Rat, Rooster and Rabbit. These are the symbolic representations of love and romance for one alliance group of animal signs.

In the horoscope, they are referred to as Peach Blossom Animals and the presence of their image in the home of the matching Alliance of Allies brings *Peach Blossom Luck*, which symbolizes love and romance.

The Tiger belongs to the alliance of Tiger, Horse and Dog, and for them, the RABBIT is their Peach Blossom Animal.

The Tiger benefits from associating with anyone born in the Rabbit year, and will also benefit from placing a painting or image of a Rabbit in the East corner of the house.

The Tiger's Peach Blossom animal is the Rabbit. Displaying a Peach Blossom Rabbit enhancer in the East will attract romance and marriage luck into the Tiger's life.

6. SEASONAL TRINITY

There is another grouping of animal signs which creates the four seasonal trinity combinations that brings exceptional luck of *seasonal abundance,* which usually manifests as wealth luck. To many astrology experts, this is regarded as one of the more powerful combinations of animal signs. When it exists within a family made up of one parent or both parents with one of the children, they will collectively be strong enough to transform the luck indications for the family members.

ANIMAL SIGNS	SEASON	ELEMENT	DIRECTION
Dragon, Rabbit, Tiger	Spring	Wood	East
Snake, Horse, Sheep	Summer	Fire	South
Monkey, Rooster, Dog	Autumn	Metal	West
Ox, Rat, Boar	Winter	Water	North

The Tiger, Rabbit and Dragon belong to the Seasonal Trinity of Spring.

This means that even when the annual indications of the year may not appear favourable, the existence of the seasonal combination of animals within any living abode can transform the luck of the family, making it a lot better. The best times will always be felt by the season indicated by the combination.

It is necessary for all three animal signs to live together or to be in the same office working in close proximity for the pattern of prosperity to take effect. For greater impact, it is better feng shui if they are all using the direction associated with the relevant seasons. Thus the seasonal combination of Spring is East, while the seasonal combination of Summer is South.

The Tiger belongs to the seasonal combination of Spring, a combination which further strengthens its links with the Rabbit, which is the Tiger's Peach Blossom Animal. When a Tiger and Rabbit marry and they have a Dragon child for instance, the three of them creates the Trinity of Spring. This means that they are not only exceptionally close but attract the luck of abundance during the beautiful season of Spring! This is also the best season for them to start anything important.

ANNUAL CHANGES
to the Horoscope Compatibilities

Everyone's energies, mood, aspirations and tolerance levels change from year to year. People tend to be more or less tolerant, more or less magnanimous or selfish, more or less distracted or warm depending on how they fare during any year.

When things go smoothly, one is better disposed to others, and even between two animal signs who are naturally antagonistic, there can still be good feelings, enough for two unlikely animal signs to enjoy each other so they can become at least temporary lovers!

Likewise, when one is being challenged by problems, that is when even the slightest provocation can lead to anger energy erupting even between secret friends, allies and soul mates. That is when friends can become short term enemies!

Compatibility between animal signs must thus take into account time periods. In this section, we look at how the Tiger person interacts with the other animal signs in the year of the Boar 2019.

Interpersonal relationships can alter drastically from year to year, so it is useful to understand underlying annual energies that affect the way we interact with others during the course of every New Year. So many aspects of the luck equation affect our attitudes, behaviour and responses to our colleagues in the work environment, to siblings within the family, to our parents and to our close friends and everyone dear to us.

When we understand why we are the way we are each year and how the feng shui luck "numbers" affect us, and we know how to deal with these energies, then life becomes a lot more pleasant, much less stressful and can even transform our overall luck.

At work, when we appreciate how the astrological elements, compatibilities and "numbers" affect our own sign of the TIGER, we can improve interactions with all others much more effectively. More so when we are also aware of how the feng shui chart and stars of the 24 Mountains affect our interactions with each other. This is about love and friendship and how we can best work with those who become dear to us. This part of the TIGER book for 2019 is hence of great importance to our well-being.

Every year, the pattern of new energies affects the way you treat people; these in turn determine how they treat you. Interactions with those closest to you are always affected by your mental, emotional and physical state. How you get on with your partner, your spouse, parents, children, siblings, relatives and friends are affected by your mood and wellbeing this year.

These relationships create important inputs to your happiness. So annual compatibility readings are an important component of your luck situation. Your relationships are also a vital dimension of your happiness.

Those born under the sign of the TIGER generally live very well. They have natural authority and instinct that comes across majestic and regal. Tiger people have very classy taste in activities, work and friendships.

In 2019, the Tiger exhibits greater ebullience and enthusiasm than its usually reserved self. The Tiger's charisma appeals to those wanting to climb the social ladder, so you always attract your own group of pals that you hang out with. Your Zodiac allies, soul mates and secret friends find you beneficial to be friends with and your popularity also rubs off on them. People like your natural leadership energy and encouraging demeanour, which is very much evident this year as your life force and spirit essence are at very strong levels. Many of your friends benefit from their relationships with you directly and indirectly. This will thus be a socially active year for you.

In 2019, the Tiger brings out the best in many of its good friends, so it will be a pleasant year. There are also invitations from new friends. This year the Tiger will encounter helpful people who bring new opportunities your way. There will be a particular introduction that will change your life. You could also meet with a powerful mentor, which is like encountering *qui ren*, helpful people who open new directions to love and success. They will mentor the younger Tiger, bringing sound advice and excellent introductions.

When your day-to-day interactions are pleasant, they strengthen your luck. Enjoying good relationship luck adds much to your well-being. But should you fall prey to jealous people, you must stay watchful and alert, especially when good things are happening for you.

The Tiger sign has the *Star of Illness* in your home sector of Northeast, a sector you share with the sign of the Ox. This can make you vulnerable to minor health issues developing into serious disorders. The illness star can cause the older Tiger to suffer from severe afflictions affecting the shoulders, limbs and back this year. Those who are diabetic must be extra careful. Do monitor your sugar levels to be on the safe side.

Note that the Tiger's life force and spirit essence are very strong, so by placing the necessary cures and wearing protective amulets, you can experience a relatively smooth year.

Another good indication for the Tiger is that you are sitting on the *Star of the Heavenly Seal* which brings cosmic protection against illness-bringing nagas. Unfortunately the Tiger's location has the star of the *Yin House* next to it; this indicates you should have yang energy-producing type placements near your location to suppress *Yin Spirit Formation.*

Definitely it is worthwhile to make the effort to focus on these different aspects of your personal and home luck. Cosmic afflictions affect how you get along with others, they influence your personal feng shui luck and knowing what to do will improve your overall annual luck.

Irrespective of what your personal luck indications may be, you must not underestimate the influences of astrological and feng shui afflictions in the important rooms of your home. These are not difficult to subdue when you know what to look for and how to pacify whatever afflictions you find.

Knowledge is key. It shows you what you can do to cope with daily differences that may crop up between yourself, your family and friends.

Afflictive energies definitely cause problems; troublesome stars create obstacles, so do make sure you get a copy of our **Annual Almanac** and **Feng Shui Diary** this year to know all the "stars" and numbers of each week and month.

HERE ARE SOME QUICK TIPS

to enhance the quality of all your relationships. Use animal sign astrological combinations to soften inner hostilities, suppress outer quarrelsome tendencies, and use knowledge of astrological stem and branch combinations to protect all your important relationships, that of your children and loved ones.

- Improve ties with your spouse. **Use his/her astrological "secret friend".**
- Strengthen bonds with your boss/colleagues. **Use astrological "ally groupings".**
- Wear the bonding **Lock Amulet** to strengthen relationships with your children.
- Bring out the best in all your friendships. Hang our "**friendship**" amulets.
- Reduce misunderstandings with your astrological enemy. **Use "their secret friend".**
- Avoid hostility turning nasty. Check #3 star afflicting you. **Use FIRE chi.**

The annual energies affect the way you respond to people; they affect your personal affinity with others. Sometimes you can feel an inexplicable aversion to someone you may have always liked or even loved; or feel attraction towards someone you might have found to be previously annoying! Our moods and our responses to people change over time.

The **69 year old Metal Tiger** and **45 year old Wood Tiger** enjoy good wealth luck and this puts you in a happy frame of mind; you feel like embracing your loved ones. Luck and life brings success and good fortune your way hence your attitudes towards most people will be positive.

The **33 year old Fire Tiger** is in the pink of health and vitality. You are also in your prime so your personality also tends to be upbeat. The only problem this year is that the Tiger's *lung ta* is very weak. There is little or no success luck and this will cause you frustration. For some of you then, anger energies can flare up, especially in APRIL this year and in JANUARY of 2020.

POWER OF ANIMAL SIGN PLACEMENTS

Usually placements that "activate" the affinity of astrological groupings, secret friends and trinity of allies' groupings as well as soul mate pairings of the Zodiac exert strong influences. Also note that annual energies can increase and decrease these influences although placing the relevant signs near you will go a long way towards making you feel good.

For the Tiger, it is best to have the secret friend the Boar nearby, and also your allies the Dog and Horse. Having the animal signs standing above a bejewelled element pillar brings excellent energies that generate powerful bonding energy for you, your friends and your loved ones. You can be more or less warm towards others depending on how elements and the numbers of the year's Lo Shu square affect you in this Year of the Boar. This is the year of your secret friend, so for the Tiger, this means you benefit from having the Boar nearby – it activates not just good energy for you but also all that is beneficial from the year.

Also, because you have the *Star of Heavenly Seal*, all the vibrations around you are amiable so your attitude towards even your zodiac enemy the Monkey is cordial. The year is however challenging because you do not feel well most of the time due to the presence of the *Illness Star* so sometimes even the slightest provocation can cause you to flare up. This depends on the way you interact with the other signs.

We examine the TIGER's personal relationships with all twelve signs in 2019.

TIGER/RAT *Outside interference*

In 2019, Tiger and Rat are compatible

The Tiger has powerful vitality while the Rat is very amorous this year, making this a potentially strong, compatible pair, but the Rat has a roving eye and is tempted to take advantage of the Tiger's illness star. In a love relationship, and in even in a marriage, an outside third party might cause problems.

Tiger is feeling extremely strong in 2019 despite the illness star affliction. The 24 Mountain Constellation brings the *Heavenly Seal*, the stamp of heavenly approval. Cosmic energy for the Tiger is thus powerful, but the Rat significantly has the romance star and might be unfaithful!

This is complemented by Rat's strong love star; thus, despite there being very little in common between their interests, they feel sympatico with each other this year. But it is a superficial pairing. The aspirations of the big cat and the tiny mouse are at two ends of a long pole, and yet, when these two get together in 2019, sparks do get ignited; they enjoy time together and find common ground.

★★

In terms of vitality, the Tiger has greater and more active life force. Younger couples will be perkier and enjoy one another more, while older pairings of Tiger and Rat discover synergy this year. In 2019, the Tiger's inner essence continues to be stronger than that of the Rat. This is excellent for the pair as it suggests the Rat can take comfort in the Tiger's reassuring energy.

The jealousy of others will not disturb these two. It is the infidelity of one of them that can cause problems. Jealousy rears its ugly head when external distractions cause one of them to fall prey to the temptation of others.

If there is third party interference, it will likely be coming from the Rat as this sign has the love star of *Peach Blossom*. This Year, Rat is afflicted by the *Star of External Romance*. This is the main area of potential conflict that might pull apart what is otherwise a compatible relationship.

Best protection against third party interference: Definitely a good idea to wear the **Marriage Saver Amethyst pendant** or carry the **Rooster with Fan**, as prevention against infidelity is better than cure.

TIGER/OX *Discovering each other*

In 2019, either can take a joyride

There are no special astrological ties between these two signs, except that both share the same home sector of Northeast and are equally afflicted by the illness star of 2019. But love and attraction can grow between two people when their life force and spirit essence are at very high levels – as these two signs are.

Tiger and Ox are very different, in that one is represented by an animal who comes from the wild, while the other is highly domesticated. The symbolism of these two signs is telling, especially in describing their different temperaments and personalities.

These two signs will usually not feel any great chemistry with one another, but in 2019, both are filled with great enthusiasm. Except that Ox is flying high with powerful *lung ta* that will make it view the year differently from the Tiger. The latter's *lung ta* is very weak indeed!

Neither sign is feeling especially romantic. For the Tiger already married to an Ox partner, it is a pleasant year to discover one another more deeply; there is enough tolerance and there is good energy flow. If this does not happen, there is risk of one getting involved in an external love relationship. This is the danger of 2019 and it is better to safeguard against anything negative from manifesting.

Protect against infidelity: It is beneficial if each wears **anti-infidelity** or **anti evil-eye protection** jewellery. As both possess strong life force and spirit essence, their own energy will empower the symbols of protection.

The good thing is that apart from the illness star, there are no other afflictions, so at no time will there be any adversarial energies between them. It is also a Boar Year, and because the Boar is the secret friend of the Tiger, there is a pacifying energy that emanates from the aura of the Tiger.

The Ox is much better focused than the Tiger in 2019, but this is a year when Tiger sits on the "*Seal of Heaven*" which brings a very special kind of luck that manifests from heaven energies. It is thus easy for Ox and Tiger pairings to do well together, whether in a love relationship or even as business partner.

TIGER/TIGER ***Equally enthusiastic***

In 2019, weak lung ta affects their moods

The Tiger has great vitality in 2019 but there is a certain frustration that impacts their mood and this is due to their very weak *lung ta*, the energy of their personal Windhorse. Tigers can be highly volatile and have low tolerance levels when things do not work out their way. The Tiger personality can be authoritative and bossy as they are natural leaders, but success luck proves elusive this year. This is sure to affect the couple when both are afflicted with the same sort of luck energies.

But as a couple, they understand each other only too well. They will be tolerant of one another's impatience and frustrations. With lack of success, there will also be a lack of triumphant excitement that fuels their interest in each other. In 2019, the main thing about this pair is one giving in to the other.

The Chinese often say that "in any hill, there can only be one Tiger." If one can give way to the other and be comfortable with the pecking order thus established, their relationship will be more than smooth and pleasant.

There are two kinds of Tigers for whom 2019 can hold out some excitement; the pair of **69 year old Metal Tigers** can look forward to a great year with plenty of prosperity luck – for them, life takes on rosier hues with some grand financial windfall to look forward to. The **45 year old Wood Tigers** also have a good year, so they too have an exciting time.

The other lucky Tiger pairing will be between two **33 year old Fire Tigers** whose vigour exceeds all other Tigers. Health luck is superior in 2019 and this means there is strength and the right attitude to go seeking for adventure and opportunities and actually finding them. The Fire energy of their heavenly stems interact beautifully with the synchronised elements of the year, bringing prosperity luck and making 2019 quite an adventure year.

Tigers are mindful of social status and can be snobbish. They get along better when both come from similar social and educational backgrounds. Tigers will get involved in a love relationship, but usually have a better relationship when both have similar starts in life. Tigers rarely change their stripes; they rarely marry down!

TIGER/RABBIT ***Heavenly chi***

In 2019, mentally and spiritually attuned

These two signs mirror each other and in 2019, their connection is strong as they enjoy heaven's blessings. They are much in tune mentally and spiritually as the Tiger is blessed by the *Star of Heavenly Seal* while the Rabbit has the #6 *Heavenly Star*. Tiger and Rabbit thus have a powerful spiritual connection that gets emphasized in the year of the Boar.

They are very much in sync and both signs are at their peak in terms of life force and spirit essence. Elementally then, they are extremely compatible; walking and running to the same rhythm, and sharing thought processes that reflect similar attitudes.

Their strong connection also arises from their *Season of Spring* connection, which is astrological. And because both are intrinsically Wood element people, they will always be instinctively mindful of growth energies. Creatively, they are looking skywards and upwards and are much in tune with each other. This reflects in many things they do together.

★★★

The Tiger is always drawn to anyone belonging to the sign of the Rabbit and vice versa. And in 2019 when the Tiger has a special relationship with the sign of the year and the Rabbit is fed by the Water energy of the year, both signs benefit. This means that both are in a position to take fullest advantage of their luck energies this year. It does not matter much then that both have weak *lung ta* this year is weak.

LUCK ENHANCER: Both benefit from carrying and displaying the powerful **Windhorse**.

When Tiger meets Rabbit for the first time, they are sure to feel a special kind of intuitive connection. Their first impressions may be superficial and may not initially indicate anything special between them, but go deeper and their inner cosmic chi will start to flow and blossom for them both. Love then grows. These two also make good business partners as they both take the long term view and look for growth.

If they can find themselves a Dragon, such as a Dragon image or better yet, if they have a Dragon child, they will form the seasonal combination of Spring, bringing wealth luck.

TIGER/DRAGON *Ho Tu*

In 2019, getting along beautifully

This is a year when the coming together of a Tiger and Dragon will reflect their celestial relationship with each other. One is *Yin* and the other is *Yang*, one is the Green Dragon and the other the White Tiger of feng shui symbolism - and this makes it a powerful pairing indeed.

We should also take note that in 2019, the respective star numbers flying into their home abodes in the year's Lo Shu square reflect the powerful Ho Tu combination of 2 and 7. This is the Ho Tu that brings wonderful wealth and prosperity vibrations for the pair. It is hence a very auspicious pairing.

Both signs also have very high levels of life force and spirit essence. They are fired up with energy and vitality. The Tiger's level is stronger than the Dragon's, but having such a good match of energy levels brings the promise of a very fine year for both indeed. These two signs benefit very much from the presence of the **Water element** around them. This makes them connect at much deeper levels and brings about wonderful growth energies that make the relationship grow strong and stable. In 2019 these two can seize the moment and start the year with a loud show of solidarity and closeness.

SEASONAL TRINITY: Their astrological luck gets even more magnified if they can add on the **presence of the Rabbit** either as symbolic image or as a sibling or child in the relationship. This generates the *Trinity of Spring*, which attracts prosperity and growth opportunities.

The Tiger and Dragon pair can achieve anything they set their minds to. They work hard. The only danger is that they can become consumed by excessive energy. This can happen in 2019 because Dragon and Tiger are both strong personalities and their intensity can work against them. Hanging **sacred windchimes** can be helpful.

This is not a year to reap the harvests of hard work. This is a year to get things started. Be mindful that the *lung ta* of both are weak; so there are obstacles to success. But have fun aiming high and enjoy the ride to success; take this attitude and this will surely be a happy year.

TIGER/SNAKE ***Mismatched energies***

Resentment and misunderstandings in 2019

This year the Tiger is at a complete loss when it comes to interacting with the Snake. A relationship with those of this sign can definitely be better and should they set aside their different viewpoints, the year can turn out very profitable and beneficial for both indeed.

The chi energies of the year between Tiger and Snake appear to complement one another, with Tiger supplying plenty of go-ahead energies brought by its excellent life force and spirit essence, and Snake supplying the success-bringing *lung ta* brought by its very good Windhorse levels. On the surface, the element energies of this pair appear in sync, but in reality, this unfortunately is not quite the case.

Why? Because the Snake does not have the energy levels of the Tiger. The Snake is weak, has low life force and weak spirit essence and thus prefers to slow down the pace. There is a mismatch of vitality levels. So in spite of their Ho Tu combination (7 and 2), the feng shui energies that should bring them together has no chance to get ignited.

★★

In 2019, the Snake will just exhaust the Tiger if they try to make things work. The Tiger is full of verve and spunk, seemingly energized by a new kind of vivacity and joie de vivre. This puts Snake in the shade, resulting in Tiger feeling impatient and Snake feeling inadequate. As a couple, they will be forced to confront a big divide developing between them.

The effect is that mistrust arises, triggered by even the smallest of things. Tiger feels that Snake is holding it back, while Snake feels vulnerable. Misunderstandings flare up frequently. It looks like it could be a sad & disturbing year for this pair.

The Snake usually slides away from conflict, as it is not in its nature to face off any sort of direct confrontation; besides, it is feeling weak this year. The Tiger finds it difficult to subdue feelings of umbrage and antipathy.

Those in a marriage who find their energies and expectations very mismatched might feel inclined to give their relationship a rest this year; each doing their own thing and not allowing resentment to fester.

TIGER/HORSE ***Patience gets tested***

In 2019, facing setbacks together

The Tiger feels instinctively protective towards the Horse, who is its astrological ally. In 2019, Horse goes through a year when it is very low indeed in life force and spirit essence. It is weak in terms of vitality and vigour, but it is also quarrelsome as it comes under the influence of the afflictive star #3. The year is extremely challenging for the Horse, so the Tiger involved with the Horse might not have the patience to stick around.

Nevertheless, these two signs are kindred spirits who can weather trials and tribulations together. They have the ability to laugh their way out of difficulties, viewing setbacks and successes with equal candour. They share a sense of adventure that enables them to create their own private world. So they understand one another and feel good about being their real selves with each other.

Between them runs a special kind of trust that Tiger cannot easily find with others. Thus it is likely that in spite of problems facing Horse, Tiger will be right by the side of its astrological ally.

★★★★

Theirs is more than a physical thing! There is a deep and spiritual connection here which takes the way they feel towards one another to a very high place. In 2019, the Tiger will instinctively feel sympatico with the Horse. In this year of the Boar, Tiger is in a very strong place. It is a time when its shoulders can be broad and comforting for the Horse.

Surprisingly, this year it will be the Tiger that does the chasing, but it may not last the course, as Horse is in a finicky mood, always quarrelling and always finding fault.

While Horse cares deeply for the Tiger, in 2019, it is hit by the *quarrelsome star #3* and this makes it impatient and intolerant, and easy to anger. Much then depends on whether Tiger is able to ignore the regular misunderstandings that are sure to arise.

Tiger and Horse belong to the alliance that includes the Dog. Together they are "the hunters" of the Chinese Zodiac, known for their patience stalking prey; in real life this applies to their amazing tenacity when coping with setbacks.

TIGER/SHEEP *No resilience*

In 2019, feeling tested amnd challenged

Tiger and Sheep enjoy similar luck profiles in 2019. Both have very strong life force and spirit essence, although here the Tiger's vitality exceeds that of the Sheep. This parallel matching of their outer and inner forces can cause them to be drawn to one another this year. However, these signs have very little in common and it is not easy for warm or intimate feelings to arise between them.

The year itself is not very encouraging as both signs have weak *lung ta*, with that of the Tiger being weaker than the Sheep. There is thus no success luck to add any excitement. Instead, there are only setbacks. Hence in terms of vitality, the year of the Boar is not particularly conducive for this pair to come together. The energies of the year work against them.

The big problem facing this couple is the affliction of the #5 star affecting the Sheep's feng shui location in 2019's Lo Shu square. The #5 is a star of misfortune, and it brings bad luck in the form of illness, difficulties and problems. It is tough for the Sheep to be pleasant as there will be

★★

tension in the air, hardship and even heartbreak. This is the affliction of the *wu wang*, which brings troubles and disasters. The Sheep's horoscope elements are very weak, so it lacks the strength to cope.

Tiger will not respond well to Sheep's unpleasant countenance this year. Faced with any kind of challenge, the Sheep will walk away as it is not up to challenges this year. In Tiger's eyes, Sheep is far too conservative and lacking excitement. The truth is that these two signs do not know how to touch each other's buttons, so passion simply cannot arise.

In the eyes of each other, neither can measure up, so it is more advisable to split than waste each other's time. The longer they stay together, the worse it will be. As siblings, they are also unlikely to be close.

Sheep's subtlety will be lost on Tiger, one being a creature of the wild, the other domesticated and considering itself more "civilised". This is not a good match.

TIGER/MONKEY *Growling*

Adversaries going their own way

In 2019, Tiger and Monkey will continue bristling at each other. This is a pair of astrological enemies who are creatures of the wild. Their innate tendency is to be naturally hostile to each other. But in 2019, Tiger is growling into thin air while Monkey will most likely swing away.

In this relationship, it is always the Monkey who will call the shots, so for the Tiger, in spite of your very strong life force and spirit essence this year, you are not strong enough to pin down the Monkey.

So if you, the Tiger, wants to develop a love relationship with someone of the Monkey sign, be prepared for a rough ride. It is no mean feat for you to win over this wily sign. For sure, you will bristle with antagonism each time you get rebuffed, and this will happen a lot. Plus this year, the Monkey suffers from the *Five Yellow* affliction, the misfortune star which brings a variety of challenges. It makes Monkey moody and harder to get close to. In terms of its inner strength and outer life force, it is at neutral levels, hence given a choice, Monkey prefers to ignore adversarial-type situations and relationships. The Tiger is no match for the crafty Monkey. Better to engage the remedy to suppress the #5 star to soften the cool indifference of the Monkey.

CURE: Carry the **Tri-coloured Five Element Pagoda amulet** to provide instant solace. Using this feng shui cure goes a long way to removing adversarial energies. In addition, also display the Monkey's secret friend, the **Snake**. Place a small image of the Snake sitting on an **element pillar** to create a more harmonizing atmosphere between you.

Some believe the Tiger/Monkey match possesses underlying currents of affection so that for them, the line between love and hate is very fine; the secret being that should they have two children born Boar and Snake such that the family unit forms the rare combination known as the *Four Elements Cross* comprising Fire and Water, Wood and Metal. Such a family will then have two pairs of secret friends; this combination spells great wealth and prosperity ahead.

TIGER/ROOSTER *Formidable pair*

In 2019, providing excellent life force to Rooster

The Tiger and Rooster can be thought of as the Cat and the Bird – two signs that are amiable (or deadly) depending on the quality of outside forces and energy affecting them. In 2019, Tiger is filled with excellent vitality, full of confidence and brimming with enthusiasm – all attributes the Rooster (the bird) admires and lacks in 2019. But Rooster is blessed with a strong personal Windhorse that enables it to fly very high indeed. As a couple, this pair can be formidable in 2019.

The Tiger provides excellent life force and inner confidence to boost the ambitious Rooster, who in turn inspires the Tiger to soar and aim high. These two are not natural enemies, but they are also not natural friends. In 2019, their underlying sentiments are positive. Both want victory and success, and the Rooster sign's indications provide it with astrological underpinnings for success.

The Tiger is also clever, not easily fooled; both have their own agendas but there is unlikely to be betrayal. Fortunately for them this year, both set aside their egos to achieve mutual goals, especially if they are a committed couple. These are individuals that are protective of their own, so if they are family, this year will be a good one.

If there is any tension between them this year, it will be because of competitive tendencies intruding into their relationship. This is where danger lies for them.

Neither Tiger nor Rooster has a long fuse, being naturally impatient; so they need to work at submerging their competitive inclinations so that tensions do not simmer into big misunderstandings. Hang the **Victory Banner**!

In 2019, the Rooster is riding very high, having a solid good year. It benefits from the *Star of Victory*, the winning star that brings triumph, and in its element profile, Rooster has a very good personal Windhorse that brings success. Tiger's success luck is not impressive, but it has a strong life force and spirit essence. This has a bearing on their roles within their relationship. As strong-willed individualistic people, they will natrally carve out their respective roles. But the authoritative Tiger and proud Rooster must sort out their ego issues to live happily together this year.

TIGER/DOG *Friendship & love*

In 2019, good vibrations all the way

This is a year when having strong life force and spirit essence can make all the difference to those with weak *lung ta* luck; Tiger and Dog play out this kind of scenario. Both are strong physically and mentally, and even spiritually. It is a year when friendships get tested, but these are allies of the Zodiac that stay true to one another.

Tiger and Dog enjoy each other's good vibrations. They support each other finding in one another a true and trustworthy friend. For a start, Tiger will discover Dog to be as dependable and as loyal as ever, Dog in turn will find that Tiger can be relied on when the going gets rough. Their allegiance to one another stays steadfast in what looks like a year that will not be entirely obstacle-free.

The Tiger in 2019 is vulnerable to the *Illness Star* but has a strong life force. But Dog enjoys the powerful #9 star in the year's feng shui Lo Shu, thus enjoying the magnifying effect of all the good luck stars it encounters, especially in the months of April and January of 2020 (*sum-of-ten* combination), in June (when the #8 flies into the NW) and in August (when the 6 flies in).

★★★★★

The auspicious influences of these star numbers get magnified and Tiger with its excellent spirit essence can benefit from the reflected aura of Dog's good vibrations. Those married to one another will find that simply by standing together, they can stand very tall indeed! This is because in 2019, the two signs have strong energy levels.

There is genuine love and understanding between these two and the good thing is there are no competitive issues or other pressures to cause tension.

This is a naturally happy pairing of two extroverts who make friends easily. They make a great team in business, as can transform seamlessly from friends to business partners. Over time, they build a network of influential and meaningful contacts. Working together brings them closer. They have high principles and strong bonding takes place at deeper than normal levels.

If they can add a symbolic image of their other ally **the Horse** and display nearby, their union becomes even more auspicious.

TIGER/BOAR *Secret friends*

In 2019, a great year to indulge

The Tiger has a natural easy-going relationship with the Boar, and in 2019 when there will be few distractions, this pairing has each other's undivided attention as befits the year's energies.

Boar has the vigour and stamina to keep up with Tiger's inclination towards active and sporty activities. They discover the beauty of the planet together as they take off and travel - hiking, skiing and dancing their way through the year. It is a year when they can indulge and have a satisfying time together.

They find one another's company exhilarating as their horizons expand. In this year of the Boar, their time together is spent mainly on outdoor activities with both having the stamina and vitality to explore together. So interactions between this pair in 2019 will tend to be physical in nature; not for them poetry reading and other sedentary activities. They also do not enjoy exploring their minds too deeply. They are happiest when going deep sea diving and mountain climbing and it is through physical activities that they discover new and stimulating things about each other. This

★★★★★

way, the year brings pleasure and good health vibrations that manifest in a much loved up way. It is not a year of great business or scholastic success, but if they engage in competitive sports, they might well feel the exhilaration of winning. The Boar is in its own year, so the powerful God of the Year, the Tai Sui is supporting it, bringing cosmic blessings its way. The Boar also has the magnifying star number 9, which is the symbolic numeral for future prosperity.

But the *lung ta* of both signs is weak this year. Both benefit from displaying the mighty red **Windhorse** as this brings them success luck.

The best thing about the Tiger and Boar pairing is the feeling of assurance they each bring to the relationship. They have no hidden agendas and are not childish in the way they interact. Theirs is a very straightforward relationship and a lifetime commitment is definitely possible for them. Those who have just met should take their time allowing their feelings to grow while they enjoy their energies. Those already married and settled into their comfort zones can indulge themselves silly this year.

Chapter Four

TIGER'S MONTHLY HOROSCOPE FOR 2019

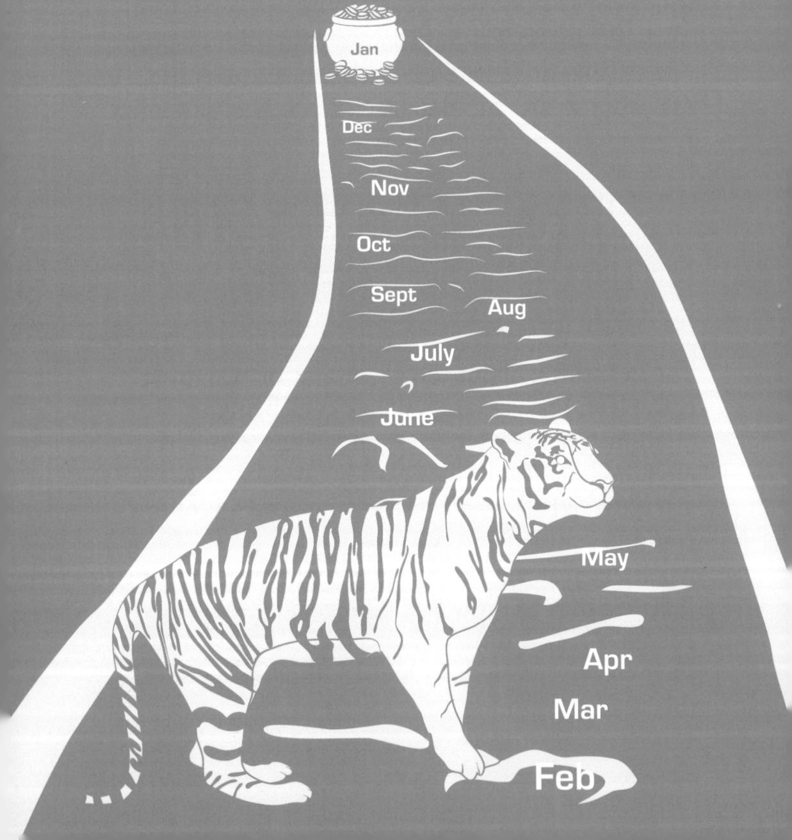

OVERVIEW OF THE YEAR

A year when patience pays off

This is a year with its fair share of good fortune opportunities for the Tiger, but also one where it pays to take it slow and to bide one's time. Resist your instinctive impulses to react instantaneously to everything that happens to you; always take a moment to think and to plan. You enjoy excellent indications in your element luck charts but lack the *lung ta* levels that bring easy success. This indicates you have to work for your achievements - but this is no bad thing as it will make your victories sweeter and more meaningful.

The Tiger features as always in the year Paht Chee, but 2019 also features its secret friend the Boar, and its astrological ally the Horse. This indicates friendship and ally luck for the Tiger, but you also have the Monkey, your astrological "foe" in the chart. Your luck is thus a mixed bag, but with moments of brilliance.

Go after what you want and keep focused, but refrain from taking too many risks. Move one step at a time and clock up minor successes building up to the big ones as you make progress. Don't fall prey to get-rich-quick schemes, which not only will not work, but could lose you a lot of money. The Water Tiger needs to be wary of financial matters.

Your most auspicious months fall in August, September and October.

The 24 Mountains Constellation brings you the *Heaven Seal*, which indicates you can trust your instincts. It also brings mentors, benefactors and helpful people that can open doors for you.

LUCK ENHANCER: The Tiger enjoys the luck of the *Heaven Seal* brought by the 24 Mountains. This brings you *qui ren* luck, the kind where you benefit from helpful people putting their weight behind you. Having powerful mentors and benefactors in your corner is always beneficial, sometimes even more important than having the skills, the talent or the drive.

This year the Tiger should activate this kind of luck by carrying the **Qui Ren Amulet** and by displaying the **Qui Ren Plaque** in your home sector of NE.

Use this monthly guide to make the most of every month. Some of you will be more lucky than others, but if you know how to navigate your luck, used in conjunction with the *Feng Shui Almanac* and *Feng Shui Diary 2019*, this chapter will show you where you should be putting your focus from month to month. It will show you when you need to lie low, when you can advance with confidence, when you should hold your tongue and when you can speak your mind.

There are rules when it comes to planning major events - and what constitutes "major" will differ from individual to individual. But events for which timing is crucial include weddings, births, grand openings, starting a new job, interviewing for a new job, having an important conversation, making a presentation to win a bid, competing in some competition, taking an exam...

But what if you cannot choose the timing of your "important date"? There are ways to mitigate less than stellar timeframes if you find yourself faced with no choice, and we include this where applicable. As far as possible, try always to be guided by this month-by-month planner to ensure highest possible chance of success and to minimalise obstacles arising to make life difficult.

FIRST Month

February 4th - March 5th 2019

Beware the Five Yellow

The first month of this Boar Year brings the *#5 Misfortune Star* into your sector, warning you to be careful. The *Five Yellow* brings unexpected and unforeseen obstacles to whatever you're currently pursuing, and has the tendency to interfere with all the best laid plans, so it is always important to subdue the #5 star whenever it appears.

IMPORTANT TIP

This month, keep the Northeast of your home quiet - avoid playing loud music or entertaining friends in a rowdy manner in this sector. If you find things in your life starting to go awry, make sure you have this year's **Tri-Coloured Five Element Pagoda** installed in this part of the house. Also adviseable to carry the portable Tri-Colored Five Element Pagoda talisman.

LUCK CHANGES QUICKLY AT WORK

You may find yourself in a vulnerable position at work. Luck changes quickly, and from everything going smoothly, things could start going wrong. This month you cannot afford to make mistakes or offend the wrong people. Harmless offenses like getting to work late or leaving early could turn into bigger issues. You could become a target for someone you have angered in the past.

MAKE ALLIES NOT ENEMIES

Resolve differences where you can. The more allies you have on your side, the better. Remember, you don't have to like someone for them to be an ally. If you don't let yourself get personal, you could even become friends with the enemy. Don't let your ego be the cause of your downfall. Recognize when it is better to give in than have your way.

AVOID RISK-TAKING

Not a good month for taking risks. A time for consolidation and taking stock of what you have on hand. Check on existing inventory rather than contemplating getting more stocks. Do not attempt entering into new ventures or partnerships, even those that seem fail-safe. This is not the time to take more than one step a time. Save cash; cash is king and you may need it sooner than you think. Time to conserve and try to offload as much as possible. Focus on selling rather than buying, as big expenses may crop up.

IN LOVE... GIVE EACH OTHER SPACE

You may face hidden tension in your relationships. Big fights may sprout up from innocent squabbles. Don't let jealousy get the better of you. Accusing your partner of flirting with others will only drive you further apart. This month, giving each other space will do you both a world of good. Pour your energies into other things if your love life isn't working out right now. You may be feeling emotionally vulnerable, but overanalysing your mental state will just drain you, or worse, scare your partner away!

WIDEN YOUR CIRCLE

If you suspect your current circle of friends are not giving you the moral and spiritual support you need, perhaps you should widen your social group. Making new friends will lift your spirits and add some zest into what can easily seem like a humdrum life. If you are feeling stifled, break free by going the gym or taking to the running track. Or plan an impromptu trip abroad somewhere you've never been before.

SECOND Month

March 6th - April 4th 2019

Excellent for the Tiger in school

This month favours the young student Tiger and anyone looking to improve themselves in terms of knowledge or skills. Study and research yield exciting findings, allowing you to make excellent progress. The Tiger has a flair for communication this month, so those in jobs that require good oratory skills do very well. All writers, scholars and students benefit from the energies of the #4 star.

LUO HAN FOR EDUCATION

Display the **Luo Han with Qi Lin** in your living or work space to boost *Scholastic* luck and make the most of the energies of the month. Those taking exams will benefit from the image of this Saint of Philosophy. His image will also aid those who have to make important life decisions.

BENEFICIAL TO NETWORK

The energies of the #4 star favours relationships, making this is a good time to cultivate rapport with your boss or superiors. Your mind is in a calm state and you are extremely dependable and easy to talk to. Use this time to make friends and network to further your position at work. You'll be adept at sorting out problems, and your organizational skills are first rate. You can offer to do more than you're currently handling; this way you are given the chance to impress and to show what you can do.

DESIGNING A MASTER PLAN

If you're involved in the media or creative industries, you're in for a great time! Dare to be different. Voice your ideas and then act on them. This month you can truly transform your vision - taking it from your head to the drawing board. But make use of your connections. Your master plan will work when you spend effort designing and putting together an effective team.

EMOTIONALLY ATTUNED

This month you feel attuned to peace, love and polishing up relationships. Because you are on the right track in your career and other commitments, you have more time to focus on your emotional needs. Watching a romantic movie with someone you like or going along with the other dating rituals will bring clichéd but tangible joy into your life. Right now you believe there's so much more to life than just working hard and making money. And there's nothing better than having someone to share your new revelations with.

MARRIAGE PROPOSALS

A good time for proposals and marriages. If you've been with the same person for a long time, this month you get to see whether you're meant to be together for life. If you feel no magic, it may be time to go your separate ways. And if you're already with your soulmate, you can feel confident in making the commitment to take things to the next level.

SOCIAL BUTTERFLY

Your social life is extremely hectic and doing the rounds seems almost like work! But you thrive on being welcomed and appreciated for your sparkling presence. Singles are in for a marvelous time. Since you are footloose and fancy free, there is no holding you back!

THIRD Month

April 5th - May 5th 2019

Quarrelsome but fruitful

Good is infused with bad this month, when blue skies get tinged with black clouds. But a roller coaster ride means you can still come out ahead if you play your cards right. One good thing leads to a less good one, but it comes back in cycles, so try and always stay a step ahead. The only consolation is that you do get things done. Projects get finished on time and within budget. You can't complain about poor sales, and revenues are as predicted. So really, the bottom line is not awashed in red ink despite your personal setbacks.

To play safe, keep a low profile, avoid self-publicity and steer clear from grey areas. You can be held liable by law if things go wrong, so check with lawyers before you sign on the dotted line. More so if it involves your personal affairs like loans or borrowings.

BETTER WORKING SOLO

Not only is work challenging, but it is fraught with possible delays unless you rein in your temper and be less argumentative. You tend to alienate others and force them to retreat, taking along their goodwill that can facilitate your tasks. Instead of criticizing or passing the buck if something is amiss, why not admit your mistake? Others are not so judgmental so why should you be? Best is to work relatively alone and only co-relate with others when you need to. You perform better as a soloist this month! Too much mingling is counter productive and impressing the boss is even harder.

NEED TO COMBAT THE #3

The quarrelsome chi makes you difficult to get along with and causes all kinds of misunderstandings in your life. Suppress the quarrelsome chi by carrying the **Peace & Harmony Amulet** and by displaying 6 smooth **Crystal Balls** on your desk or in your home sector of NE. Also place the **4 Seasons Tree of Life Red Carpet** in this area - this is the best antidote against the #3 star.

TOUGH MEASURES

Not a good time for partnerships or joint ventures. Success rates are low. Instead, focus on human resources. There may be some instances of fighting and backbiting among your staff which can lead to stalled work and lowered production. You have to intervene, mediate and if necessary perform drastic surgery by deciding who has to go.

BEWARE LOVE TRIANGLE

If you wish to have a harmonious life, avoid a triangular affair! Whether you're married or involved in a steady relationship, a third party may enter, severely upsetting the equilibrium. Since you are the one holding the key, the ball is in your court whether to nip it in the bud or allow the illicit affair to bloom. Married Tigers easily get exasperated with their spouses but this is no excuse to look elsewhere for succour. Be more tolerant of their failings since you are not perfection personified either.

FENG SHUI CURE: Place an **amethyst slab** under the bed and tie it with red string. If things really threaten to derail, wear the **Marriage Saver Medallion** with Amethyst and Rooster.

FOURTH Month

May 6th - June 5th 2019

Health worries; energy levels flagging

Last month was stressful, but this month is hardly better as you now have health worries. You are particularly susceptible to viruses doing the rounds, so take extra care. Don't drive carelessly and avoid rough sports since your defences are down and you are liable to injure yourself for no good reason. If you can, avoid long distance travel as moving from place to place attracts bad energies for you. Wear the **Travel Protection Scarf** or carry protective **amulets** if you have to travel.

Some money losses are indicated but if they are small amounts, write them off mentally. Donate to charity to improve the odds against you. By willingly giving away your money, you churn up better luck. Ultimately, lying low and maintaining quietude may be your best option.

CALLING ON FAVOURS

Your career is not going great guns but is not slowing down either. You need to develop closer relationships with those you work with daily. Success comes from having support and allies who believe in you have never been more important, so get cracking building those bonds. You may be forced to call on a few favours, but there is nothing embarrassing asking for help, so go for it. Some may be only too willing to return the favour since you may have helped them previously.

WEAR GOLD

You suffer some form of lethargy and listlessness and should wear **gold jewellery** to offset this dilemma. Set reasonable targets you know are achievable; don't burn yourself out slaving away. Work smart, not overly hard. Working with no fixed deadline will bring out the best in you as the thought of having to complete within a given timeframe could unnecessarily stress you out.

POOR WEALTH LUCK

Wealth luck is down so it is tough trying to generate sales. Deals are difficult to close and you must work doubly hard to make the same amount of money! Nothing comes easy as you sadly prove, but if you persevere, you can still come out ahead. New projects seem shady, and unless you know the background of the promoter, it is best to shy away.

Avoid radical pursuits or short cuts. What seems too good to be true usually is! So keep this adage to heart. This is a terrible time to invest as the more money flows out, the worse it gets, since returns are unpredictable.

A BETTER LOVE LIFE

Your love life is infinitely better than your professional life, which is some consolation! If you can't have everything, make the most of what you do have. Your partner is a bedrock of support and the one who will lend moral and emotional assistance, so do confide your worries and problems to them. Share your thoughts, dreams and ideas with each other. Take comfort from their advice. Your better half also has some very good suggestions you can put into practice right away. This illustrates the importance of having a loving, caring partner who is always there for you in your hour of need. Show your gratitude with a token of appreciation; some flowers or his/her favourite meal.

CALLING ON FRIENDS

You need good friends now, so call old friends and acquaintances just to say hello. Ask for advice if necessary and it will be gladly given. Single Tigers have a good time and if you are scouting for a partner, you may well find someone you can consider a soulmate, so now is a suitable time to hook up.

FIFTH Month

June 6th - July 6th 2019

Coming out tops!

Your luck takes a turn for the better and good luck arrives by the containerload this month! Now is the time to take things easy, put your feet up and rest your weary head! As your luck improves, some big changes are also heading your way. They are for the better so there is no need to worry. This is a month of new beginnings so you can expect many new things. Previous efforts from months past bear fruit now and you stand to reap a bountiful harvest.

The future becomes clear and what you can see seems exciting and full of happy prospects. Certain things may not go the way you plan, but if you look at the positive side, you will realize it is only a matter of perception and you are still on the right track.

BUSY AS A BEE AT WORK

As busy as a bee at work, but you thrive on it since the new challenges are right up your street and you can handle them with aplomb. You may be transferred to a new department, get a pay raise, get promoted in some form or receive a new portfolio. Some new colleagues may join your section or you have to handle a new project. Whatever is thrown at you, take it in your stride. You can be hugely successful - all you need is to perform as usual. This time your talents and efforts will be noticed and appreciated. You can impress the boss and your leadership potential comes to the fore. You may even be asked handle more people or subordinates, so here is another chance to prove your people skills. You are confident and assured of your talents, so think positive and it's all systems go!

FENG SHUI ENHANCER:
The *Victory Star #1* brings you all manner of good fortune. Better if activated, so carry the **Victory Banner Amulet** or display one on your desk. This will help you win over the competition whether at work, in business, at school or in life in general.

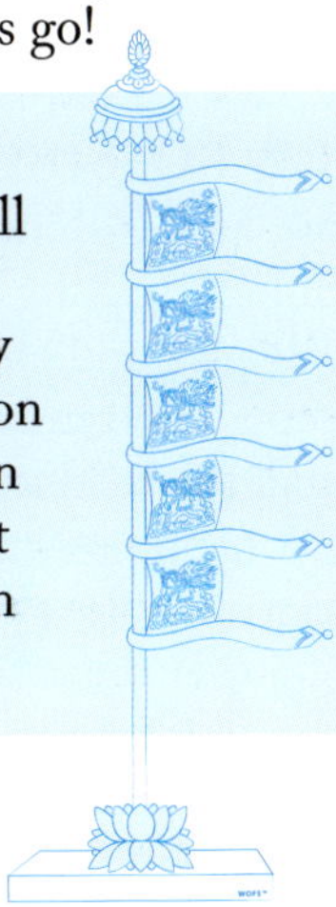

You have more responsibilities thrust upon you, but nothing you cannot handle. This month allows you to shine, so exploit all situations where you can claim your deserved credit.

LEADERSHIP QUALITIES

You appear to be a natural born leader this month. People look up to you and that includes important entrepreneurs from other firms! In business, you think up new ways to increase sales and cash flow and most of your ideas are workable. But you may be so engrossed with petty issues that you forget to see the big picture. Don't lose sight of bigger potential in the medium term for instant small returns now.

NEW POSSIBILITIES IN LOVE

Love luck is shining on you and there are many admirers arriving on your doorstep. You can really pick and choose for once! If you have been disappointed in love lately, this month makes up for all the lackluster affairs of months past. There is great happiness in store in the near future; this can mean a fabulous night, relationship or engagement. Whatever the case, it's an occasion to celebrate!

TIME TO SPRING CLEAN

A great time to spring clean the house and restore everything back to its original splendour. If you are too tired, lazy or pressed for time, hire a professional cleaner to do the job. The end results will make you look forward to returning home at the end of a long work day.

SIXTH Month

July 7th - Aug 7th 2019

Fast-moving & full of energy

You bubble with energy and life seems there to be enjoyed to the max! You are at the right place at the right time and you have the right attitude. But in your glee and extravagance, try not to overspend. Hidden expenses may crop up that involve huge expenditures you have not anticipated, so conserve as much cash as possible.

You feel inspired and whatever you are putting your energy towards succeeds easily. You may occasionally feel like you're stretched too thin, but the thing is, the busier you are, the quicker you get things done. You thrive on full-on days with a packed schedule. In fact you're more likely to feel out of sorts if you don't have enough on your plate. Having said that, do watch you don't burn yourself out. Your resident *Illness Star* gets magnified by the #9 this month, which while pumping you with energy also makes you susceptible to falling ill, or collapsing with exhaustion.

Get enough sleep each night and wear the **Wu Lou** or **Garuda pendant** to keep sickness energies at bay. Learn to pace yourself.

DEPEND ON YOURSELF

At work, things may not always go to plan, but you have the capacity to cope. Depend on yourself. Think up your own strategies rather than ask too many people for their opinions. Trust your own judgement and instincts. You're still full of self-assuredness, which allows you to impress your views on others, swaying them over to your way of thinking. Others believe in you and you are very persuasive. Just remember to believe in yourself!

FAMILY ARGUMENTS

At home, things may not be so harmonious. There are some harmony issues fuelled by your hyper energetic mood and a possible mismatch of energies between you and other household members. This will be especially the case if some of your family members - especially siblings - are born under equally strong animal signs. Tiger-Dragon clashes for example, can be particularly severe; so if you have a Dragon within your household, watch you two don't butt heads too often.

PLAYING MEDIATOR

You may have to intervene and play the role of advisor/mediator if there is friction between family members. You seem able to take the lead in most familial situations and they listen to your views, so play fair. Be jovial and cheerful; a smile and laugh is infectious and may be just the right antidote to chase away the blues. Rustle up a family dinner get-together and stay away from sensitive topics over dinner-time conversation.

SOWING THE SEEDS OF LOVE

Single Tigers have a big appetite for love this month, but frustratingly you may be so busy you don't have sufficient time to capitalize on this. Don't fret. Make your conquest wait a little. You'll have more time on your hands next month. This is a month to sow the seeds; love will not grow and blossom till next month, so be patient. Drop small hints you are interested, but don't overwhelm your target of affection with too much attention. Keep up the mystery if you want the magic!

YOUNG TIGER FEELING STRONG

The Tiger in school/college has plenty going on but feels fully ready for anything. If you can learn to focus, there's little you can't achieve. High grades, the respect of your teachers, the admiration of your peers are all there for the taking. But if you just party or while the time away, you may enjoy yourself but not have much to show for it.

SEVENTH Month

Aug 8th - Sept 7th 2019

Wealth & Completion Luck

Probably your best month this year. You enjoy the arrival of the current prosperity star, which is also the wealth star, but more than that, it combines with the resident #2 to form a *sum-of-ten*. A really auspicious indication which gives you the ability to complete things, bring projects to fruition, close deals and get to the finish line. This month you see the culmination of all your hard work, when you reap the fruits of your harvest.

Enjoy and continue seizing all the opportunities that come your way! Your run of good luck holds strong for the next three months, so you can be confident about taking risks or venturing into unknown or unfamiliar territory. Money-making opportunities abound and is especially strong for the **69 year old Metal Tiger** and the **45 year old Wood Tiger**. The young **21 year old Tiger** just starting out also enjoys promising prospects.

ENHANCER: Carry the **Treasure Box Amulet** or call on the help of the Wealth God with the **God of Wealth** keychain.

PROMOTION LUCK

There's promotion luck at work in one way or another. This may be as simple as getting extra responsibilities that you enjoy, which lead to more rewards later, or being put in charge of a glamorous new project or a straightforward promotion with pay increase! Income luck will ensure you have no cause to complain about funds. You may even be offered a partnership or stock options or a company loan with minimal interest. Even if you don't get a leg-up now, you are definitely earmarked for promotion.

A thrilling time for budding tycoons, established entrepreneurs and up-and-coming business people!

CHANCE OPPORTUNITIES

This month you encounter money-making options by chance. You could meet someone at a function who proposes some lucrative deal or buys from you. A casual chat with someone you barely know can lead to some big project. In extreme cases, you may literally bump into someone with ideas! Whatever the case, such encounters bring vast benefits and you don't even have to work for them! An opportunity unrelated to your main line of work may also open up.

BE BOLD IN LOVE

Love is in the air and everywhere you look it seems! If you have been secretly admiring someone, now is the best possible time to let your feelings show. While previously the person may not have bothered about your existence, this time they may be the one doing the chasing! Fortune favours the bold, and more so in your case now.

TIME FOR A FAMILY TRIP?

You have the funds to finance family activities and are happy to demonstrate your generosity with outings and treats for everyone. Though you make the final decisions, include everyone and try to make them seem like group decisions to avoid quarrels. Keep everyone in the loop and make them feel like a part of the decision-making. A family holiday now apart from making happy memories could yield something terrifically exciting. Time to make some travel plans!

HONOURS FOR THE STUDENT

Good fortune luck for the Tiger extends to the young Tiger in school. Your stars shine bright and you are in line to win scholarships and honours. Now is the time to prove you have what it takes to excel. As long as you are sufficiently prepared, you do very well indeed!

EIGHTH Month

Sept 8th - Oct 7th 2019

Ho Tu brings great wealth

The #7 joins the #2 to form the *Ho Tu* that brings great wealth. Continuing on from last month's *Prosperity Star*, this indicates Tiger has a good few months of an excellent run, giving you plenty of time to accomplish whatever you set out to achieve. If making money is not your priority, luck also favours those who have causes to advance, or statements to make. Those active in community service or social work can also make meaningful progress.

You enjoy a special kind of popularity where others rally around you and help you. The #7 star however has its downsides; it brings risk of betrayal and duplicity, sometimes from unexpected quarters. This month you are going to have your supporters but also your detractors. Watch whom you trust, how much you reveal and to whom.

Keep your circle small, your friends close, your enemies closer. You're on top of things if you actively stay alert and aware.

FENG SHUI CURE: Display **red-faced Kuan Kung** in the NE of your living room to combat negative intentions sent your way, protecting you against jealousy and ill intent from rivals and enemies. The month holds out bonanzas but also obstacles; if you can navigate your moves carefully, this could turn out to be a milestone month.

BIG RISK-BIG RETURNS

The opportunity to make money is most definitely there but the risks may not be worth the returns. But don't work up too big of a risk appetite, because unless you can stomach it, you could cut your losses and fold before you manage to see things through to big profit-taking. Speculating on the stock market can bring gains, but you need to think longer term if the gains are to be meaningful.

CAREFUL WHO YOU TRUST

Limit contact with people who seem dubious or whom you feel uncomfortable working with. It is better to err on the side of caution even if it means a potential loss of revenue. You have wealth luck, but potential to lose money makes it unwise to move forward when the risk factor is too high.

WEALTH ACTIVATOR

Activate for Big Wealth with a **Treasure Chest.** Fill with ingots and crystals. If you already have a treasure chest, add to its contents this month. This symbolic ritual will activate the positive aspects of the month's energies.

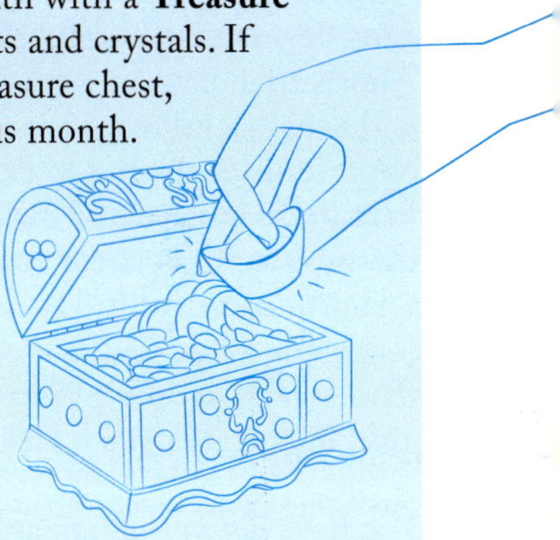

LITTLE TIME FOR LOVE

For the single Tiger, your mind is not on love or matters of romance. Other areas of life are taking up too much of your time for you to think up sweet nothings to whisper into the ear of your potential love interest. Not the best of times to try and date; your mind will probably be a million miles away, so as well as being a waste of time, it could drive your potential partners away, for good. And that would be a real shame if one was actually a keeper.

NINTH Month

Oct 8th - Nov 6th 2019

Heaven luck guiding you

Another fabulous month! So many delightful and beneficial things to look forward to. Many opportunities abound to demonstrate your talents, help those in need and make money. Now is also the time to think about charity work since money seems to come easily. Do not forget the less fortunate; know that many others may work harder than you yet receive pitiful returns. The more you give, the happier you'll feel.

You have determination and staying power, two important factors that will push you ahead of the herd. You have interesting options before you, but you can't have them all; so decide which appeal to you most and then go for them! Chances are high you will succeed quite gloriously.

MENTOR LUCK

You also enjoy mentor luck this month. Someone higher up in rank takes a personal interest in you. Cultivate this friendship as you have everything to gain from it. This person could well hold the key to unlocking all sorts of new opportunities for you, but you will have to work for it.

GOOD IDEAS

Let your creativity reign supreme and you will come out tops! Give in to your wilder ideas and see if they are workable. You never know what gem is germinating in that brain of yours. You have good ideas now, so share them with your team or boss! Work at developing good relationships with superiors; it will stand you in good stead and help you leapfrog to the next level. Cultivate such friendships assiduously.

EXPANSION PLANS

A good time to think about investment and expansion. Business luck is good and new initiatives pursued turn out well. Use the advice of friends in the know. Keep your ears to the ground to stay well-informed about market trends. Keep abreast of the news or you may miss something important. The better informed you are, the greater your chance of getting in on something that will keep you more than busy for the coming months, and in a good way.

PERSONAL GROWTH

This is a time when you find yourself capable of things you never dreamed possible. If there's something you've always wanted to try, give it a go! You're feeling fearless so if there was a time when you can make a real go of it, it is now. Look out for a mentor figure to surface in your life who can make a real difference to the speed of progress in whatever you're pursuing. This could be someone you've just met, or someone you've known a long time but only now adopts this kind of role in your life.

NEW FRIENDSHIPS

You find socializing and developing new friendships something you enjoy immensely. You are feeling more open to new ideas and your areas of interest broaden considerably, especially if you mean for them to. Go out there and make this month a journey of discovery. The best time to venture out of the humdrum of your daily life is at a time when you're feeling strong and when you have the luck of helpful people on your side. Friendships formed now promise to last well into the future if you make the effort to develop them.

FENG SHUI ACTIVATOR

Carry the **Qui Ren Amulet** to activate precious mentor luck. Who you know is more important than what you know. Attracting a suitable mentor into your life will make all the difference.

TENTH Month

Nov 7th - Dec 6th 2019

Beware the misfortune star

Better to tread carefully as your luck takes a turn for the worse. The *Five Yellow* misfortune star pays a visit and brings all kinds of obstacles. Be cautious when making decisions; don't rush head first into things without thinking. Have a back-up plan because things may go wrong. But when obstacles arise, don't let yourself be discouraged. This dip in your luck will correct itself by month's end and whatever has gone wrong will start to come right again.

FENG SHUI CURE: While the Tiger has good element luck this year, never underestimate the *Five Yellow*. It can wreak havoc in an otherwise lucky period, so do carry the **Tri-coloured Five Element Pagoda Amulet** to ensure you escape the worst of its effects. Also place one in the NE3, the sector of your sign of Tiger.

AVOID RISK-TAKING

It's one of those months where when something can go wrong, it does. Try not to let your guard down, especially if you work in a highly competitive environment where rivalry between colleagues is endemic and sometimes destructive. It could be a matter of survival of the fittest, so get yourself into the frame of mind to fight if you have to. Although you have unlucky stars in your chart, your life force and spirit essence are excellent, giving you the mental strength to battle through whatever crises you meet up with.

STAY INFORMED

A mediocre month for business. Be alert to changes in the business environment. Don't follow your instincts alone when making decisions. Try to stay as informed as you can, so you can use logic when deciding on important issues. You may have much on your mind, but this is not the time to confide in anyone or speak out. Keep your problems to yourself for now. Solutions will come to you as the bad mojo of the month gradually wears off, but letting the wrong people in on your problems could turn molehills into mountains. Avoid unnecessary expenditures or new investments - better to stay liquid in your cash. Avoid new hires or any drastic changes in strategy for now.

MENTAL RATHER THAN PHYSICAL

Things could be lot better when it comes to love and romance, but this part of your life brings you more joy than career and money matters now. Your relationships are more about developing meaningful mental bonds than anything too physical. If you have a loving partner, you will find much solace in his or her arms this month.

The single Tiger would do better laying off the dating game for now. You're not at your best, and may come across self-absorbed in conversation. You have too much on your mind to worry about impressing others, so don't even try. Focus instead on keeping your friendships. Good friends provide better company now than new acquaintances. A good time to look up an old friend.

FICKLE FRIENDS

When it comes to friendships, don't be surprised if your friends suddenly change their plans with you last minute. Although this may be aggravating, cut them some slack. They probably have good reason. You may be quite inconsistent yourself, but you're only reacting to what's going on around you. The energies this month are a little unsettling, so instead of falling out with people you care about, be more tolerant.

ELEVENTH Month

Dec 7th 2019 - Jan 5th 2020

Love & friendship luck abound

Relationships are your forte this month. You get along famously with people from all walks of life, and this will help you in your work, business and social life. You start to feel truly happy. Small misfortunes that hit you last month start to reverse themselves, and it feels like the rainbow after the rain. Enjoy yourself but instead of living just for the present, take some of your good fortune into the future by building relationships that last into the long term.

ALL ABOUT RELATIONSHIPS

This month is all about relationships. The more connected you are with the people around you, the happier you'll be. At work, learn to operate effectively as part of a team. Working with others will be so much more rewarding than trying to achieve everything on your own; this is especially true this month. You have the vibe that makes it easy for others to click with you. As long as you make the effort, others warm towards you.

You'll find yourself in the middle of all the action this month. Because you find it easy to get along with everyone, some will be tempted to use you as a go-between. When you start becoming your boss' confidante is when you know you're really going places. But don't overstep the line just because the powers-that-be seem to favour you. You could fall out of favour just as quickly if you start taking it for granted.

BUILDING STRATEGIC ALLIANCES

In business, ideas you've been working on start to blossom into reality. Look out for people you can form strategic alliances with. Partnerships pursued at this time have a good chance of working out well. The source of your wealth now is striking deals with the right people. When allocating your time, allow enough to pursue something worthwhile to conclusion, rather than try to go after too many different things. Spreading yourself too thin will wear you out with not so much to show for it.

Socializing and networking proves extraordinarily fruitful. The people you meet at functions and parties not only keep your interest, but end up more to you than just social acquaintances. Push past polite conversation and idle chatter to get to the substance. If you keep it up, you never know what gems you'll find. This is also a good time to meet up with old or long lost friends. They may bring you opportunities you wouldn't want to miss.

FENG SHUI ACTIVATOR: Carry the **Friendship Amulet** to activate the luck of beneficial and loyal friends. This month you are going to meet a lot of people; this amulet will ensure you gravitate towards those that are good and beneficial for you, and who will last as friends into the longer term.

IN THE MOOD FOR FLIRTING

If you're single, you'll find yourself in the mood for flirting, but keep your hands off those who are off limits. You don't want to become the victim of a possessive spouse or lover. Those married or attached will find pleasure in upping the bedroom activity. Spice up your relationship by making the effort to surprise your loved one. If you're in a situation where the spark is in danger of dimming, act now or infidelities could pop into the picture.

TWELFTH Month

Jan 6th - Feb 3rd 2020

Feeling short-tempered

Don't be surprised if you're more hot tempered than usual or if others find fault with you more often. After a month of smooth-sailing, someone disagreeing with you could come as a huge shock to the system. Don't let it throw you out of sync. Others are allowed have their own opinions, and, your ideas are not necessarily the best ones. When you feel your blood rising, hold your tongue and give yourself time before retorting. Take a step back to see the bigger picture and you won't work yourself up into such a state.

FENG SHUI CURE: Carry the **Red Eagle with Jade Disc Amulet** or **Anti Conflict Amulet** to neutralize the quarrelsome energies. Wearing the **colour red** will also help. Do NOT have windchimes in the NE this month- this will cause the Tiger all kinds of problems.

Anti Conflict Amulet

While you may find others difficult to take right now, others may see you in exactly the same light. Try not to be so argumentative.

REMAIN CIVIL

Getting along with some of your toxic work colleagues could prove something of a challenge. There may be one or two who will be true pains in the neck, but keeping them on your side is a better tactic than going for all-out war. There is no need to become bosom buddies, but try to at least remain civil, or a falling out could see you end up the bigger loser.

In discussions, let others finish before you pipe up. Constantly sticking your nose where it doesn't belong may leave you ending up left out of important discussions altogether. Don't let your natural curiosity be your downfall. In all, the less said on your part the better. While your ears are an invaluable asset this month, your mouth could prove a liability.

AVOID NEW PARTNERSHIPS FOR NOW

Make yourself easy to get along with. You may have to be the yielding one in any relationship, business ones included, but giving in is better than losing it all over a clash of ideas. Avoid signing new agreements or entering into joint ventures this month. Document everything in black and white to make sure you are legally protected. Don't work by honour of the word. The word could be remembered differently by both parties, leading to unnecessary unpleasantries surfacing.

BE THE "BIGGER PERSON"

Things are not all fair in love this month. Especially the case for those of you in otherwise secure partnerships. If you're married, you can be sure your better half will irk you more than ever. You have to put in a lot of effort if you're hoping for even an iota of romance. If you can be the "bigger person" and let every quarrel and misunderstanding go, you'll enjoy the month a lot more.

Another way to deal is to focus on other areas of your life and leave bedroom antics for another time. But don't rush from one pair of arms to another and do something you will regret a long time. Wear or carry the **Marriage Saver Medallion** to protect your marriage.

for more on all the recommended
feng shui cures, remedies & enhancers for

2019

please log on to

www.fsmegamall.com/2019